Dear Adan,

Hope you have a very merry Christmas and a happy new year with these German artists! ☺

Love, Shaun and Deja

MATTHEW GALE & KATY WAN

Magic Realism

Art in Weimar Germany 1919–33

TATE

First published 2018 by order of the Tate Trustees
by Tate Publishing, a division of Tate Enterprises Ltd,
Millbank, London SW1P 4RG
www.tate.org.uk/publishing

on the occasion of the exhibition
Magic Realism: Art in Weimar Germany 1919–33

Tate Modern, London
30 July 2018 – 14 July 2019

This exhibition is realised with thanks to loans from The George Economou Collection, with additional support from the Huo Family Foundation (UK) Limited

A catalogue record for this book is available from the British Library

ISBN 978 1 84976 588 6

Production Controller: Juliette Dupire
Picture Researcher: Sarah Tucker
Designed by Joe Ewart
Colour reproduction by DL
Printed and bound in Italy by Graphicom

FSC www.fsc.org MIX Paper from responsible sources FSC® C013123

Front cover: Albert Birkle
The Acrobat Schulz V
Der Akrobat Schulz V 1921
(detail, see p.23)

Back cover: Otto Dix
International Riding Act
Internationaler Reitakt 1922
(see p.28)

Measurements of artworks are given in centimetres, height before width

Unless otherwise stated, all illustrated works are drawn from The George Economou Collection or the Tate collection; for details see the list of works (p.106)

Magic Realism: Art in Weimar Germany 1919–33

SELECTIONS FROM THE GEORGE ECONOMOU COLLECTION AND TATE COLLECTION

This exhibition takes a particular view of a rich period in German art that came in the wake of the First World War and reflected a search for a new cultural identity in troubled times. The founding of the postwar republic in Weimar made reference to the enlightenment culture of Goethe and Schiller. At the same moment, the local art school was transformed by the modernist architect Walter Gropius into the Bauhaus with a specifically reformist agenda. Between these contrasting manifestations of renewal, a generation of painters came to prominence associated with a 'return' to realism seen through a modern lens. The range of artists encompassed in this development is extensive and they did not form themselves into a single coherent grouping. For all that, within three or four years of the Armistice, there was a recognition that realism could again be contemporary. In order to distinguish this from the emotional drama of expressionism, in 1925 the art historian Franz Roh named this phenomenon 'Magic Realism'. He suggested that the new vision was anchored in the recognisable, but aspired to achieve 'a magical gaze opening onto a ... transfigured "reality"'. Such a remaking of reality could be seen as a continuum of the wartime upheaval, and the fixation upon the details of modern life lay behind the term 'New Objectivity' (*Neue Sachlichkeit*) that began as an alternative to 'Magic Realism' before superseding it. However, Roh's original term – that we have borrowed for our title – retains a telling sense of the combination of the actual and the uncanny that is reinforced by extracts from the novels of his contemporaries.

The George Economou Collection, from which the majority of works in this exhibition are drawn, is especially strong in this area. Over many years the collection has been formed around a particular enthusiasm for Weimar culture and the closely related practices in Austria and bordering regions. Outstanding in this respect is the comprehensive collection of the prints of Otto Dix, from which we have been able to draw the pre-eminent satirical and inventive *Circus* portfolio of 1922. Alongside works by Dix's well-known colleagues George Grosz and Max Beckmann, are a selection of paintings by notable artists who are unjustly less well-known outside Germany, such as Albert Birkle, Heinrich Maria Davringhausen and Herbert Gurschner. For a variety of reasons (including the historical legacy of both European wars) these artists are poorly represented in Tate's collection, but the chance to draw upon the riches of The George Economou Collection offers a rare opportunity to see a small selection of key Tate paintings return to the context in which they were originally made and exhibited nearly one hundred years ago.

It would not have been possible to borrow from a single source so extensively without the wholehearted generosity of George Economou and Skarlet Smatana, the director of his foundation. It is a great pleasure to acknowledge this support and to thank them for the interest that they have shown in all aspects of the exhibition. We should also like to thank their colleague Irene Dimitrakopoulou who has been crucial to its logistics. All have shared their knowledge and enthusiasm with Matthew Gale who, with Katy Wan, has seen this project through to fruition, ably supported by Hayley McConnell and Amy Emmerson Martin. Harriet Pearson, Annette King and Alastair Johnson have provided invaluable expertise in matters of conservation and framing. At Tate Modern, Achim Borchardt-Hume, Gregor Muir and Helen Sainsbury have all offered advice. The loans have been facilitated through the UK Government Indemnity scheme, and we would like to thank the Department for Digital, Culture, Media and Sport and the Arts Council for administering this process. Finally, I would also like to thank all those at Tate who have made it possible to bring the exhibition to the public, including colleagues in art handling, communications, curatorial, development, front of house, learning, legal, media, press, registrars and special events.

It is inevitable in 2018 that the anniversary of the end of the First World War echoes down the intervening century. The uneven healing of its scars is seen in the works that artists produced in the wake of the conflict, an aspect explored in depth in the commemorative exhibition *Aftermath: Art in the Wake of World War One* organised by our colleagues at Tate Britain. In response to these complex circumstances *Magic Realism: Art in Weimar Germany 1919–33* evokes the unflinching vision that, during its short life, suited the precarious and violent, but liberal and vibrant culture of the Weimar Republic.

Frances Morris
Director, Tate Modern

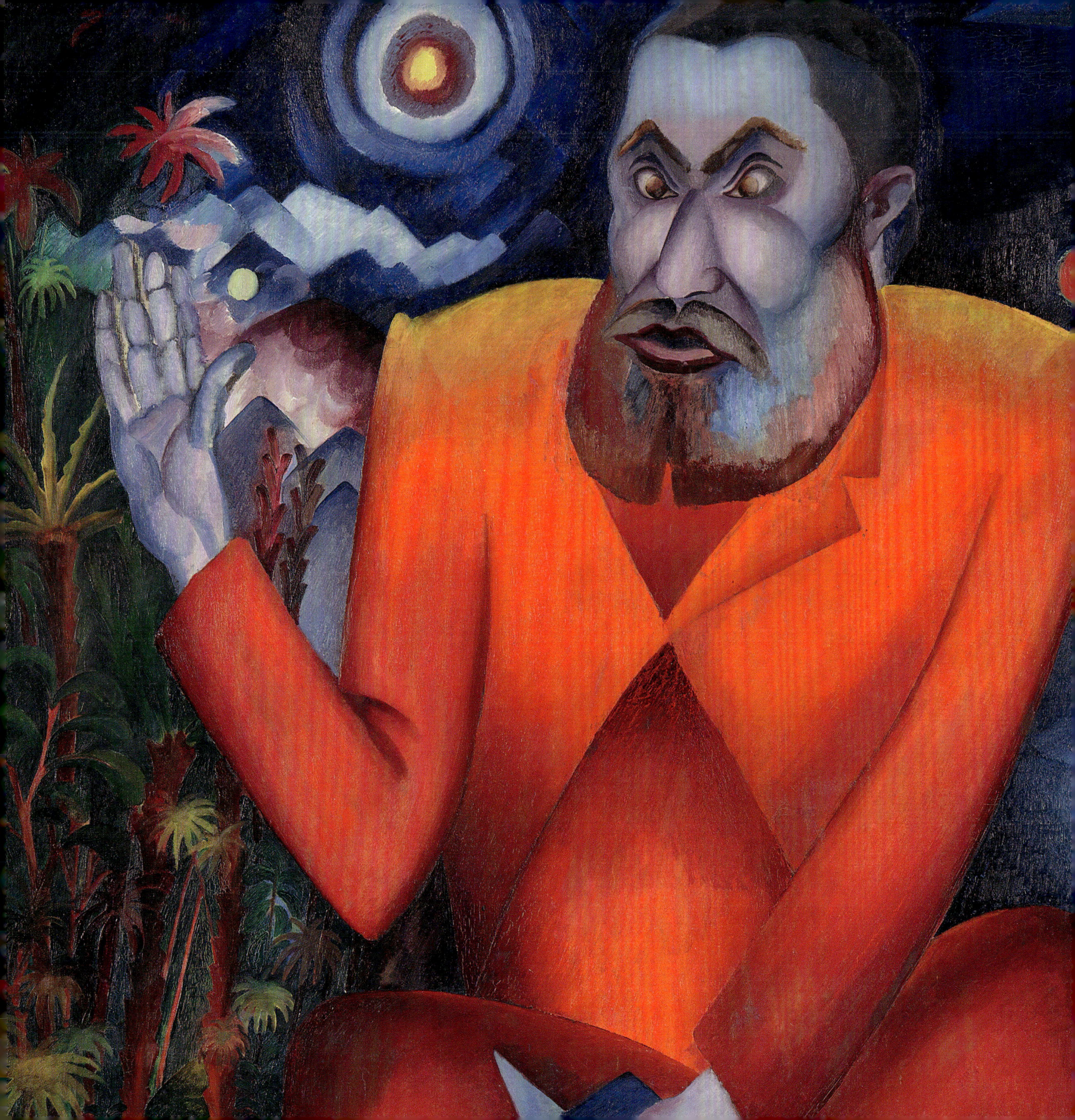

Introduction: 'The Interior Figure of the Exterior World'

It is now 100 years since Europe emerged from the Great War with the Armistice of November 1918. The continent was reshaped by the conflict: the population cut down and traumatised through loss and hardship, with social and political structures patched-up in a liberating, uneasy or vengeful peace depending on the point of view. The fortifications and trenches marked the landscape and the psyches of so many individuals as to shift the centre of gravity in the social fabric. Many artists seeking social change had gone to war enthusiastically, even knowing that they might fight their erstwhile neighbours in the bohemian quarters of London, Munich or Paris; they soon reflected the catastrophe in works bitter with the experience of bloodletting. Looking back from the 1930s, Walter Benjamin wrote: 'A generation that had gone to school on a horse-drawn street-car now stood under the open sky in a countryside in which nothing remained unchanged but the clouds, and beneath these clouds, in a field of force, of destructive torrents and explosions, was the tiny, fragile human body.'[1]

The defeated nations that had entered the war as empires – Germany, Austria-Hungary, Ottoman Turkey – were broken up in the peace settlement with the victorious countries. From centralised but multinational states emerged nations ancient and modern (Austria, Hungary, Poland, Czechoslovakia, Yugoslavia) leaving the truncated protagonists as fledgling parliamentary democracies stripped of their imperial trappings. In Berlin, Munich, Budapest and Vienna, radical communism took hold in an echo of the October Revolution in Russia in 1917, only for the bloody assertion of military authority over what was perceived as sedition (and Lenin's World Revolution) to sweep it aside. The bourgeois democracy born of war and repression in Germany had few periods of stability, and was hampered by the piercing resentment of those who had served in the army, the terrible number of wounded and incapacitated, an economy struggling to recover from conflict and the payment of reparations to the triumphant Allies. Inflation became uncontrollable, government influence was undermined and radicalism among specialist interest groups of the political right and left leached into everyday activity: the places people frequented, the associations they joined and the newspapers they read reflected all these connections.

For many painters the freedom of form and colour associated with pre-war expressionism lost its magnetism in a new postwar sobriety and cynicism. An identification

Detail, see p.11

between man and nature had suited the earlier, anti-industrial, return to fundamentals but the memories of the trenches and the failed proletarian revolutions began to make such idealism seem, in some quarters, self-indulgent. The works of artists such as Marc Chagall, Paul Klee and Heinrich Campendonk (see pp.9, 40), shown widely in Berlin and Munich, carried some of these legacies but tried to reshape them – at times taking idealism into mysticism.[2] Their visionary qualities suggested ways in which the energetic past might develop into a creative present. This inspired slightly younger artists such as Heinrich Harry Deierling, who served for three years at the front and, in recompense perhaps, seems to draw upon this visionary position in imagining the symbolic, nurturing figure of *Der Gärtner* (*The Gardener*) 1920, (p.12)[3] in vivid contrast to the recent destructiveness of human activity.

The realist trend that stuttered into life among modernists in Germany after 1920 – alongside expressionism, geometrical abstraction, dada and academicism – assumed many different names. These ranged, as we shall see, from *Neue Naturalismus* ('New Naturalism') and *Neue Sachlichkeit* ('New Objectivity'), coined by the writer and publisher Paul Westheim and the curator Gustav Friedrich Hartlaub respectively, to *Nach Expressionismus* ('Post-Expressionism') and *Magischer Realismus* ('Magic Realism'), the conjoined terms proposed by the critic and art historian Franz Roh. Across the European perspective that Roh and Hartlaub embraced this revision of avant-gardism came to be associated with the *Rappel à l'ordre* ('Return to order') aesthetics adopted by Pablo Picasso and André Derain in Paris, the *Arte metafisica* ('Metaphysical art') of Giorgio de Chirico and Carlo Carrà in Italy, as well as emerging artists in Germany.[4]

The disrupted illusionism of the Italian metaphysical painters became especially influential in Munich, where the illustrated periodical *Valori plastici*, with which they were associated, was available by 1919.[5] Paul Klee and Max Ernst came across it there independently,[6] as did Roh's circle, which included the painters Heinrich Maria Davringhausen, Carlo Mense and Alexander Kanoldt.[7] The combination in the Italian artists' work of illusionistic spaces and unsettling juxtapositions of objects embodied the uncanny or surprise. Another point of contact was through the Triestine poet Theodor Däubler, a contributor to *Valori plastici* although resident in Germany, whose remarkable

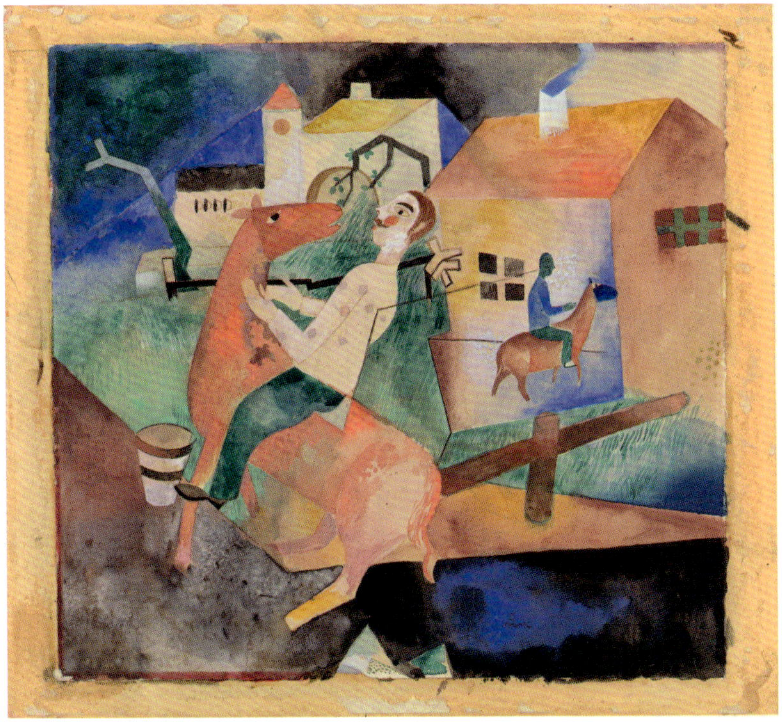

Heinrich Campendonk
The Rider II
Der Reiter II 1919
Watercolour on paper mounted on cardboard, 35.3 × 39.3

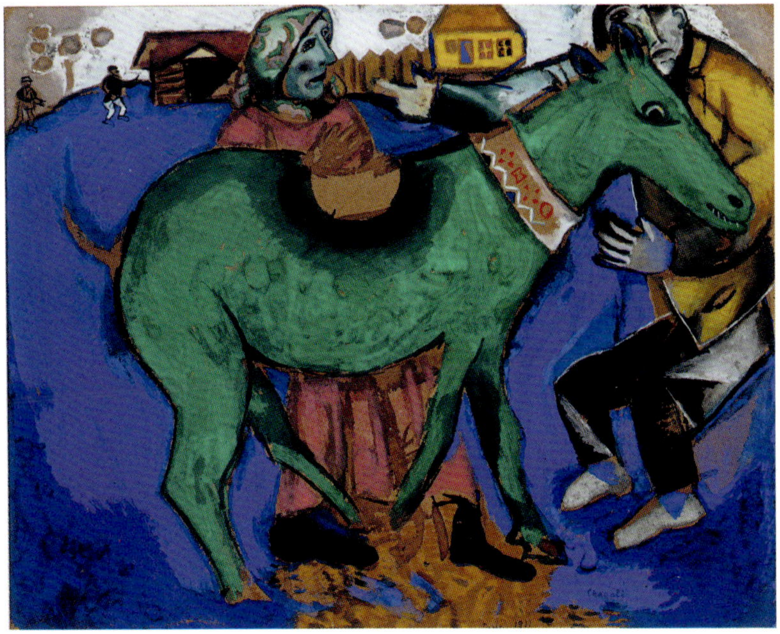

Marc Chagall
The Green Donkey
L'Ane vert 1911
Gouache on board
32.4 × 41.3

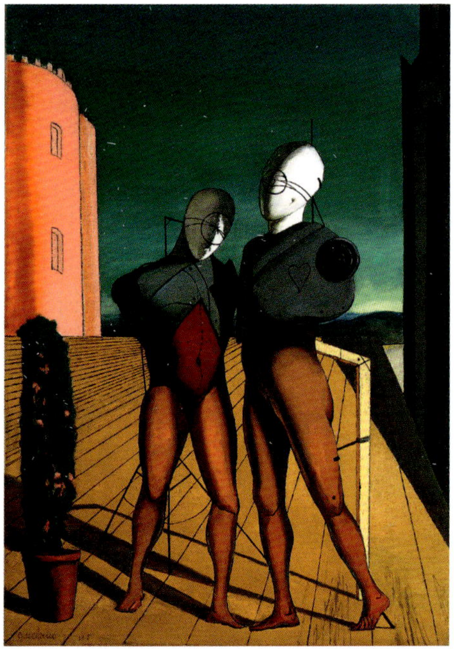

Giorgio de Chirico
The Duo 1914–15
Oil paint on canvas, 81.9 x 59
Museum of Modern Art, New York
James Thrall Soby Bequest [1213.1979]

physical and psychic presence Davringhausen captured in a grand visionary portrait (p.11). In 1920 Däubler contributed an article to *Der Cicerone*, which introduced a German-speaking audience to the mannequin figures of De Chirico's paintings, associating them with the famous stories of E.T.A. Hoffmann.[8] Very quickly, a range of artists adopted mannequins as surrogate presences and an atmosphere of dehumanisation even crept into lifelike portrayals. This interest was reinforced when the Nationalgalerie in Berlin opened an exhibition of *Valori plastici* artists in April 1921. Invited to give an introductory lecture, Däubler spoke of 'a language of intensified form amongst the youngest artists who ... aspire to create an autonomous Italian art'.[9]

The enthusiasm for *Valori plastici* did not lead to a use of the term 'metaphysical' for the new art in Germany; instead, Westheim launched a questionnaire in 1922 on the 'New Naturalism' in his cultural periodical *Das Kunstblatt*. Among the respondents, Hartlaub identified a strand that was both classicising in reference and critical in confronting 'the true face of our time'.[10] In 1923, on becoming director of the Kunsthalle in Mannheim, he began to work on an exhibition about the new art, although his plans were delayed by the restrictions resulting from the French occupation of the city in that year.[11] It is notable that this proposal also coincided with the most acute period of postwar inflation (when Herbert Bayer at the Bauhaus was designing banknotes valued at one hundred million marks),[12] and that the sobriety of the work that Hartlaub eventually included reflected the pervasive impact that this economic collapse had on everyday life. The worst of the crisis had passed by the time that the exhibition opened in June 1925 under the title *Neue Sachlichkeit: Deutsche Malerei seit dem Expressionismus* (New Objectivity: German Art since Expressionism), and over the next twelve months it travelled to eastern cities, to Dresden, Chemnitz, Erfurt, Dessau, Halle and Jena. Hartlaub gave accompanying lectures (such as that in Dessau attended by Klee), which helped to secure the term in broader usage and specifically associating it with German developments.[13] In his

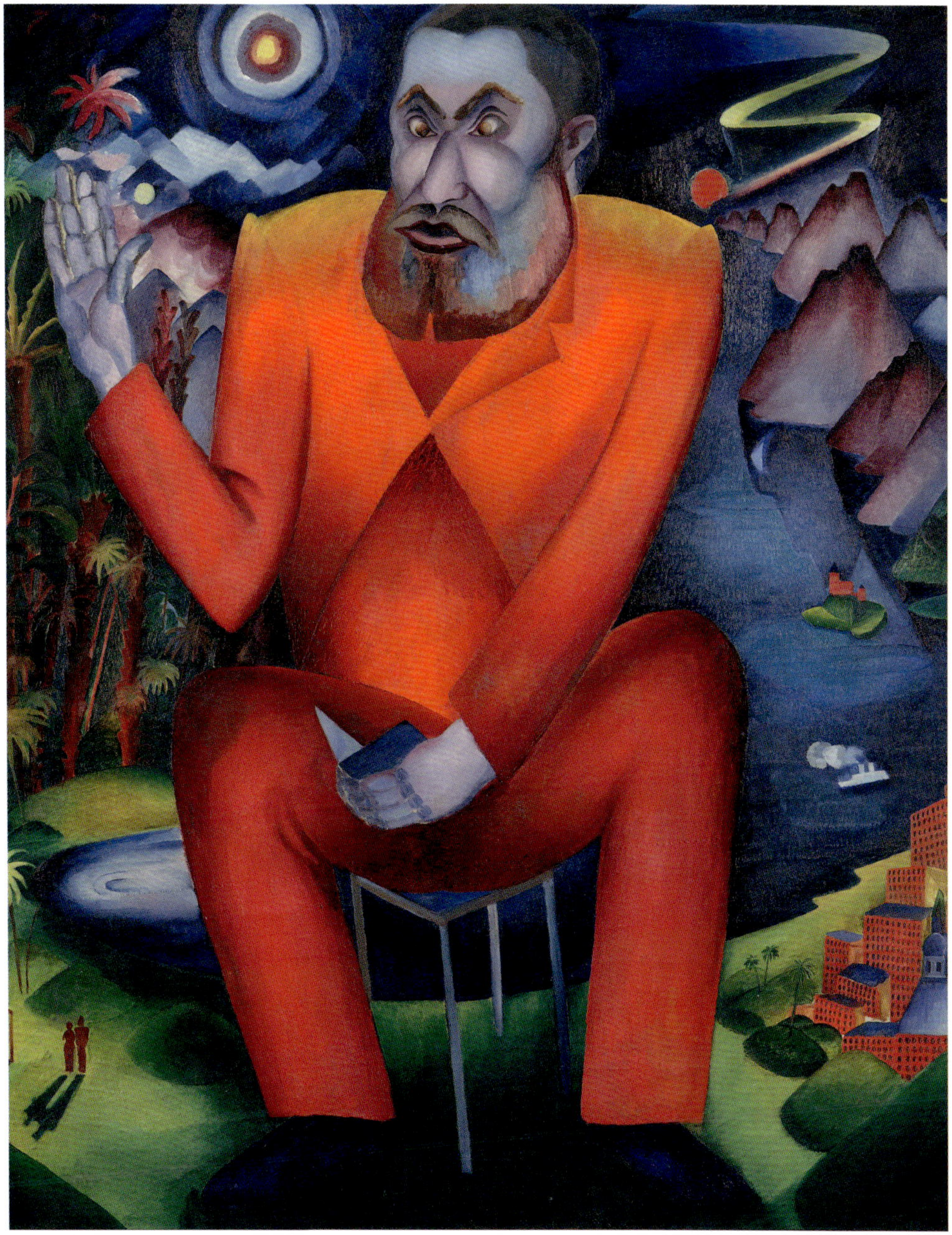

Heinrich Maria Davringhausen
The Poet Däubler
Der Dichter Däubler 1917
Oil paint on canvas
181 × 160.3

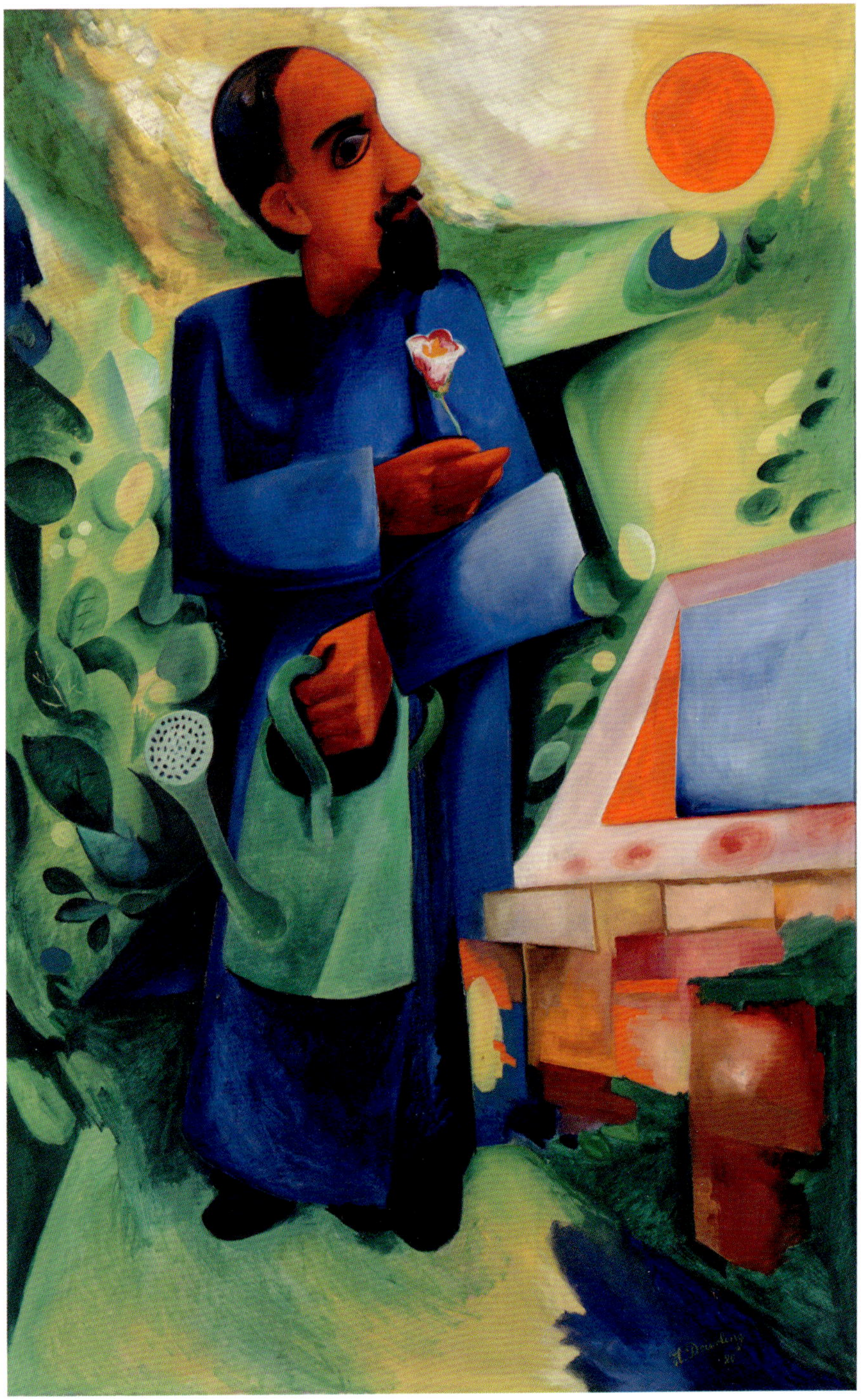

Harry Heinrich Deierling
The Gardener
Der Gärtner 1920
Oil paint on canvas
187 × 119.5

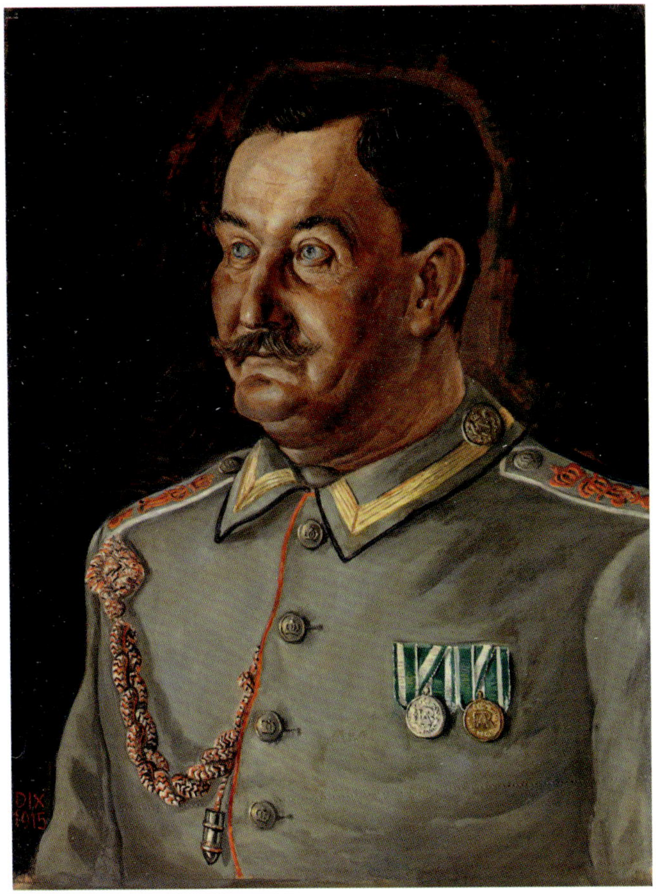

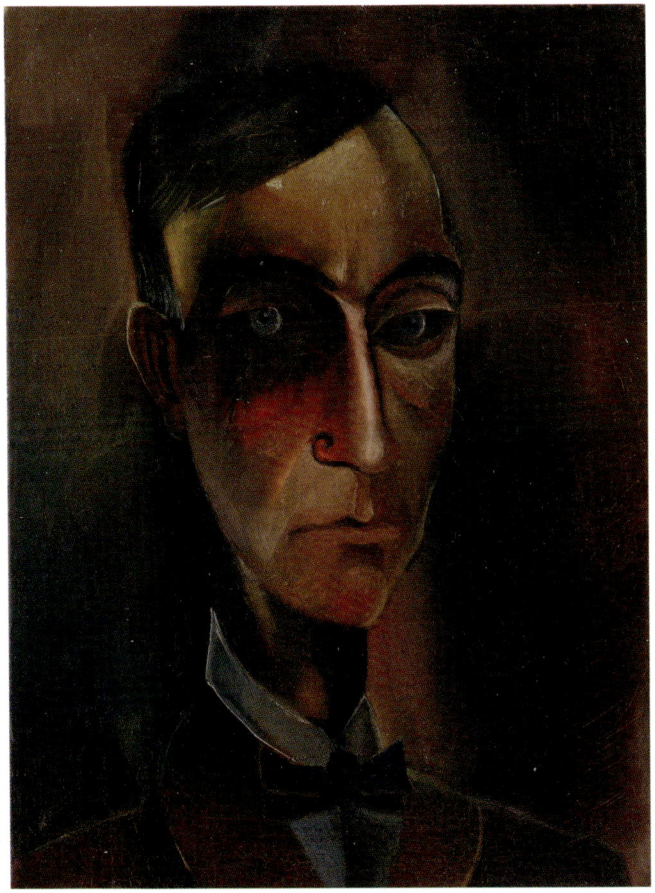

Otto Dix
Portrait of Bruno Alexander Roscher
Bildnis Bruno Alexander Roscher 1915
Oil paint on board
67 × 50.5

Carlo Mense
Self-Portrait
Selbstbildnis 1918
Oil paint on canvas
45.7 × 34.3

'... this is the worst of it, Father doesn't understand about prices nowadays ... he doesn't know that we've lost everything, and his pension will keep us for only two days in the month ... in addition, my sister's husband fell in the war, leaving her with four small children. But Father has no idea of the material difficulties we're in. At first we saved hard, even more than before, but that didn't help. Then we began selling things – we didn't touch his beloved collection, of course, we sold the little jewellery we had, but dear God, what did that amount to? After all, for sixty years Father had spent every pfennig he could spare on his prints alone. And one day there was nothing for us to sell, we didn't know what to do, and then ... then Mother and I sold one of the prints. Father would never have allowed it, after all, he doesn't know how badly off we are, how hard it is to buy a little food on the black market, he doesn't even know that we lost the war, and Alsace and Lorraine are part of France now, we don't read those things to him when they appear in the paper, so that he won't get upset.

'It was a very valuable item that we sold, a Rembrandt etching. The dealer offered us many, many thousands of marks for it, and we hoped that would provide for us for years. But you know how money melts away these days ... we had deposited most of it in the bank, but two months later it was all gone. So we had to sell another work, and then another, and the dealer was always so late sending the money that it was already devalued when it arrived. Then we tried auctions, but there too we were cheated, although the prices were in millions ... by the time the millions reached us they were nothing but worthless paper. And so gradually the best of his collection left us, except for a few good items, just so that we could lead the most frugal of lives, and Father [being blind] has no idea of it.'

Stefan Zweig, 'Die unsichtbare Sammlung', 1925, translated by Anthea Bell in *The Invisible Collection: Tales of Obsession and Desire*, London 2015, p.17

catalogue introduction Hartlaub made clear that he did not see the new art as displacing expressionism (as others did), nor did he propose to cover all tendencies (he subsequently held an exhibition of abstract art). Significantly, however, he laid out a differentiation between two 'wings' of the new art that would become habitual. Writing of a 'concreteness, in itself purely external', he drew this distinction:

> The first – one would almost want to speak of a 'left wing' – is tearing actual things out from the world of real events, evoking experience in its actual tempo, its specific heat; the other is searching for the timelessly valid object in order to realise, in art, the eternally valid laws of existence. One has been called 'verist'; the other might almost be called classicist. Both designations are only half correct.[14]

Through this encompassing approach Hartlaub was able to draw together the disparate elements but also to acknowledge the stimulus of the radical politics espoused by those 'verists' previously associated with Berlin dada, especially Otto Dix, George Grosz and Rudolf Schlichter. It was this socially critical and satirical practice that dominated accounts of his designation *Neue Sachlichkeit*, with the 'classicists' being considered more conservative, more bourgeois.[15]

Franz Roh, whose exploration of the new art had developed in parallel with that of Hartlaub, published his pivotal book *Nach-Expressionismus: Magischer Realismus. Probleme der neuesten europäschen Malerei* (Post-expressionism: Magic Realism. Problems of the New European Painting) only in December 1925.[16] As well as avoiding the term *Neue Sachlichkeit* in his text (although the publishers added it to the wrapper in order to boost sales at Hartlaub's exhibition),[17] Roh took two distinct positions that are evident from his title: he saw the new art as superseding expressionism and he saw it as a wider European phenomenon.[18] He offered 'magic realism' as a term that captured the sense of a new stability, even as it encompassed such different subjects as urban reconstruction or material poverty. The 'magical' distinguished the current work from nineteenth-century naturalism and pointed towards the uncanny within the everyday (in terms of Sigmund Freud's recent identification of the *Unheimliche*),[19] which Roh recognised in *Arte metafisica*.

In a crucial passage he commented on this autonomous art responding to the surrounding world and its conditions:

> Painting now seems to feel the reality of the object and of space, not like copies of nature but like another creation ... To depict realistically is not to portray or copy but rather to build rigorously, to construct objects that exist in the world in their particular primordial shape. The old Aristotelian idea of imitation had already gained a spiritual quality. For the new art, it is a question of representing before our eyes, in an intuitive way, *the fact, the interior figure, of the exterior world.*[20]

Like Hartlaub, Roh acknowledged a disparity between the 'wings' of the new art, noting in their meticulous techniques that: 'both kinds of miniaturist painting (the one that reconciles us to the world, and the one that tries to horrify us) imply an orientation toward the infinity of small things, of the microcosm.'[21] Most influential was Roh's schematic listing, which contrasted qualities (both thematic and technical) that he attributed to expressionism and post-expressionism respectively, including:

Expressionism	*Post-expressionism*
ecstatic objects	plain objects
many religious themes	few religious themes
the stifled object	the explanatory object
rhythmic	representative
...	
monumental	miniature
warm	cool to cold
thick coloration	thin layer of colour
roughened	smoothed, dislodged
like uncut stone	like polished metal

He concluded, tellingly, with the opposition of 'primitive / civilized'.[22]

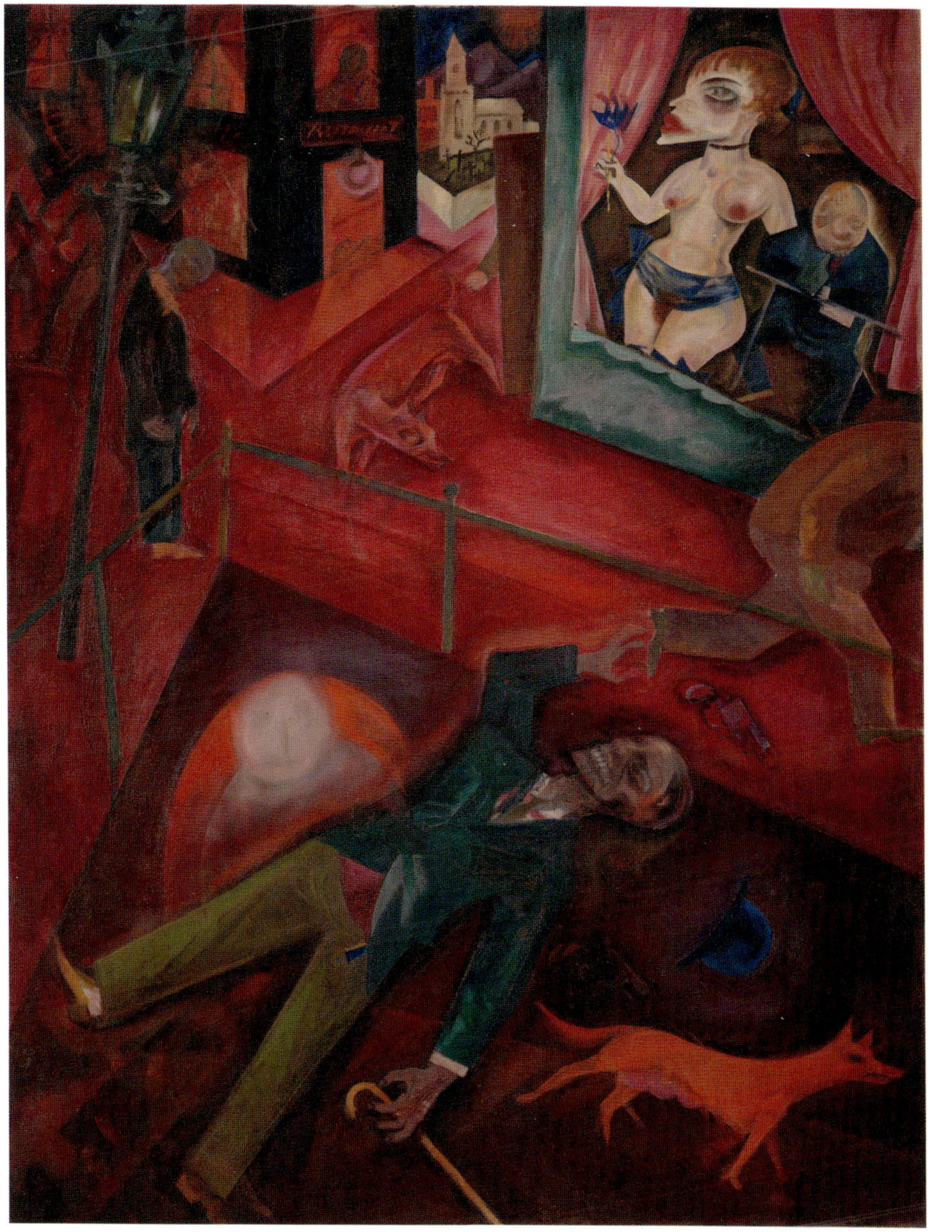

George Grosz
Suicide
Selbstmörder 1916
Oil paint on canvas
100 × 77.5

Although Roh had provided some assistance to Hartlaub's exhibition, their positions were subtly different and in some senses competing.[23] Where Hartlaub appreciated the power of the politically explosive art of Dix and Grosz, Roh favoured the classicism of his colleagues in Munich. In this respect Hartlaub's exhibition seemed to take the temperature of the crisis of 1923 – a moment pitted with the repercussions of the joint French and Belgian occupation of the Ruhr, and Communist and National Socialist risings – while Roh's book argued for the new art as an element of a centrist politics found in the stabilised conditions of 1925.[24]

The years 1924–9, that is to say those in which the new realism was most resonant, came to be regarded as the 'Golden Twenties'. They are associated with the concurrent stabilisation of the economy (bolstered by the reduction of reparations through American aid under the 1924 Dawes Plan) and the upsurge of a commercial, experimental, primarily urban, culture. The rewards of advanced industrialisation made their way into radio and cinema, while more immediate entertainments were found in the theatre and the cabaret, the circus and carnival. Magic realism flourished briefly in this period, maintaining in balance the inherent contrasts and contradictions gathered under the umbrella term. As the social and economic conditions eased somewhat, so the 'verists' took a longer view; Dix, in particular, engaged with memories of his horrific time as a machine-gunner in the trenches. An increasing investigation of an 'old master' technique led towards a convergence with more established academic traditions. This was so much the case that Christian Schad felt it took him ten years to reach his technical command, and as Dix employed fine drawing and subtle glazes so he was aware of a loss of spontaneity.

This period of growth was cut short by a catastrophic failure of confidence in the New York Stock Market in October 1929 in the fabled Wall Street Crash. Economic and political chaos returned. Bank failures followed in Germany in 1930–1, causing widespread panic and putting pressure on the government to underwrite vulnerable institutions. The threat of unemployment, inflation and reduced salaries – all of which had been characteristics of the instability of the early 1920s – returned. Communists blamed capitalist employers; racist National Socialists blamed Communists and a perceived Jewish conspiracy that built upon the (equally fictional) myth of a republican-backed 'betrayal' underlying wartime defeat. When such means became entangled with the re-election of the right-leaning General Paul von Hindenburg to the German presidency in 1932, it was the masterfully mendacious propaganda of Adolf Hitler that permeated the crisis-ridden social fabric. Wanting to believe in something, many chose to believe in the mirage that the National Socialists built on a programme of national pride, racial purity and militarism, as well as a cocktail of internal suppression and international aggression. The message may have been confused, but there was sufficient belief to edge Hitler into the chancellorship in January 1933. A ruthless construction of power was further consolidated after the Reichstag fire which was conveniently blamed on Communists and led to the banning of all political parties other than the National Socialists; on Hindenburg's death in 1934 Hitler assumed the presidency as well as the chancellorship.

It is perhaps, in part, the extreme inversion from liberalism (and liberality) to totalitarianism that continues to attract retrospective interest in Weimar Germany. From the hardship of those years came astonishing creativity that was to be snuffed out through a number of parallel lines of assault: banning and burning, sacking and persecuting, exiling, imprisoning or executing. Weimar culture collapsed. The National Socialist regime turned to realism, but the art historian Wieland Schmied has identified how the watershed of 1933 marked a distinction between 'official painting [which] consisted of a pseudo-realism, in contrast to the sharply observed naturalism of *Neue Sachlichkeit*'.[25] The extravagances of Weimar persisted only in the people and objects hidden at home or transformed by distribution abroad. Some among those identified as 'verist' artists, like Dix and Schad, found the means to work through a low-profile 'inner exile', while others, like Max Beckmann and Grosz, escaped the country. Both Roh and Hartlaub were deprived of their official positions as degenerate modernists, although they survived to review the period in their postwar work.

MG

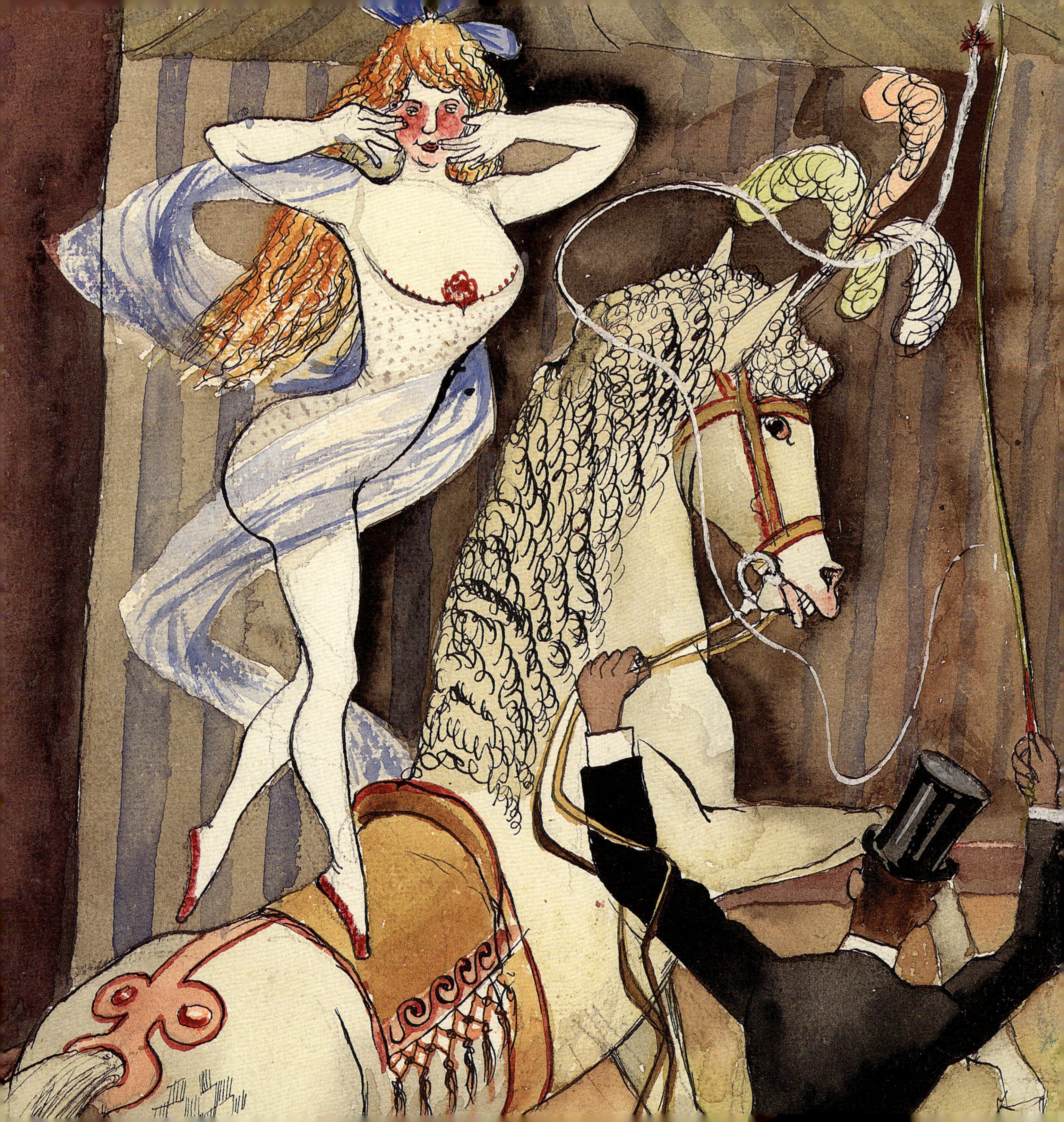

The Circus: 'Abnormal Situations'

Looking back on his wartime experience, Dix wrote: 'You have to see things the way they are. You have to be able to say yes to the human manifestations that exist and will always exist ... Abnormal situations bring out all the depravity, the bestiality of human beings'.[1]

While this view was notably given visual expression in Dix's seminal print portfolio *Der Krieg* (The War) 1924, these words might as easily apply to his approach to depicting those individuals who were considered at the time to be socially and morally transgressive, across his oeuvre. In different ways, this is seen in subjects relating to two specific themes: the nonconformist backdrop of the circus, and the violent crime of *lustmord* (sex or lust murder). George Grosz, Max Beckmann and Rudolf Schlichter were also particularly associated with these genres, which suited the cynical realism of the 'verist' wing of *Neue Sachlichkeit*, with Dix being one of its most prominent practitioners.

These two genres came to prominence concurrently in the early years of the Weimar Republic as artists sought to depict profound societal changes and transgressions. While challenging the fragile status quo, they traversed the line of society's boundaries of acceptability, particularly with regard to representations of the body and the dark impulses of human nature. These artists gave form to violations of social codes, against the backdrop of an increasingly saturated image culture, brought about by the rise of mass entertainment and external cultural influences, particularly those of the United States.

Of all the artists who expressed such themes during this period, Dix is especially notorious for his depictions of the circus and of *lustmord*. Dix's artistic practice is dominated by an almost obsessive preoccupation with physiognomy. Following in a long tradition of portraiture and caricature, the pseudoscience of physiognomy played on the belief that an individual's appearance was – or could be exaggerated to be – indicative of their personal characteristics. This sense of revelation was approached in different ways. With Beckmann, individual identity is often obscured by mask-like visages and reliance upon schematic archetypes, particularly in his depictions of circuses and carnival acts. In contrast, Albert Birkle was concerned with the remarkable physical idiosyncrasies of his sitters: in his portrait *Der Akrobat Schulz V* (The Acrobat Schulz V) 1921 (p.23), the conspicuous nose and deep-set eyes of the performer are clearly a favourite for the artist since they make numerous appearances over a four-year period.[2]

Detail, see p.33

For Dix, whether in portraits of identified individuals, such as his seminal works *Bildnis der Journalistin Sylvia von Harden* (Portrait of the Journalist Sylvia von Harden) 1926, or in his allegorical *Vanitas (Jugend und Alter)* (Vanitas (Youth and Old Age)) 1932, bodily types and features are unequivocally shown to be an expression of the individual's personality or role. This inner world of emotion and desire, of 'magic', beyond that of the empirical world and how it was manifested to a greater or lesser extent in public realms, was a repeated obsession for many artists loosely associated with magic realism.

The circus was one of these realms of public fantasy, even if it may now seem to be rather anachronistic in the context of Germany's so-called 'Golden Twenties'. The period was characterised by the rapid surge of mass entertainments, defined in part by the nascent technologies of radio and cinema. The first public radio broadcasts were heard in Berlin in October 1923. The German film industry was slightly older and, hampered by an embargo by other nations on its cinematic exports,[3] faced the challenge of American films being readily screened in German cities. Nonetheless, late expressionist cinema, epitomised by Robert Wiene's *Das Cabinet des Dr. Caligari* (The Cabinet of Dr. Caligari) 1920 and Friedrich Wilhelm Murnau's *Nosferatu* 1922, was testament to the great strides in cinematic experimentation in Germany at this time.

Against the backdrop of these augmented realities, in which mass audiences could be addressed in their own homes by politicians and poets, and bear witness to the beauty and charm of matinée idols and screen goddesses in the cinema, how could the circus compete? Perhaps an answer lay in the circus being a dynamic (and live) reflection of a fictive version of 'real' society, an exaggerated microcosm, the struggles, skills and achievements of which were detached from everyday life but strangely linked to it. This seems to be substantiated by Hans Fallada, whose 1931 novel about small-town politics and radicalisation opens with the arrival of the circus.[4] In apparent disregard of new and rival technologies, the circus flourished in these years and showed itself to be just as ambitious as a platform for showcasing a world within and beyond Weimar Germany's borders.

Unlike film, circus troupes were mobile internationally, crossing the Atlantic in both directions. The American company Ringling Bros and Barnum & Bailey Circus is a notable

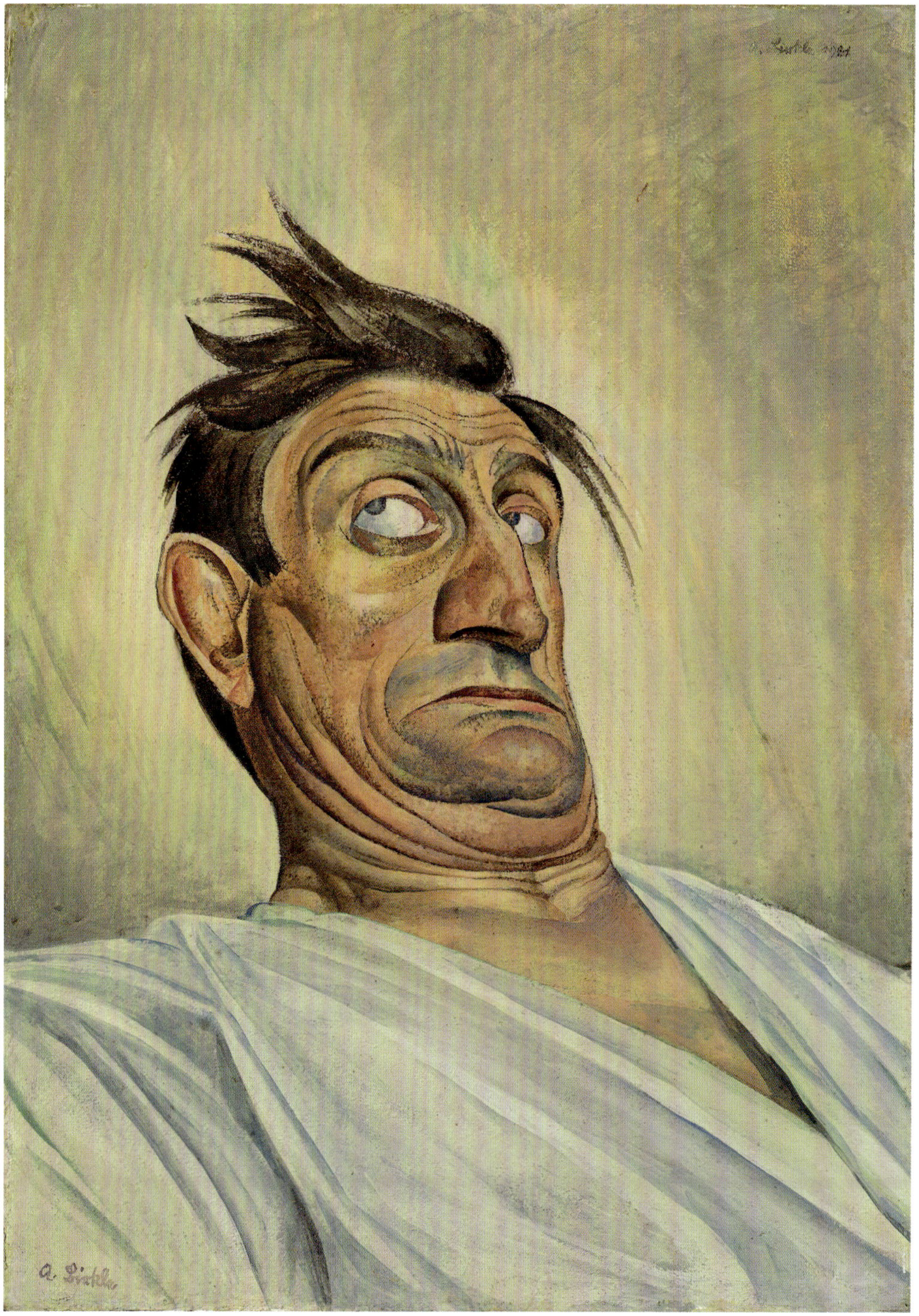

Albert Birkle
The Acrobat Schulz V
Der Akrobat Schulz V 1921
Tempera and chalk on paper mounted on cardboard
70.4 × 50

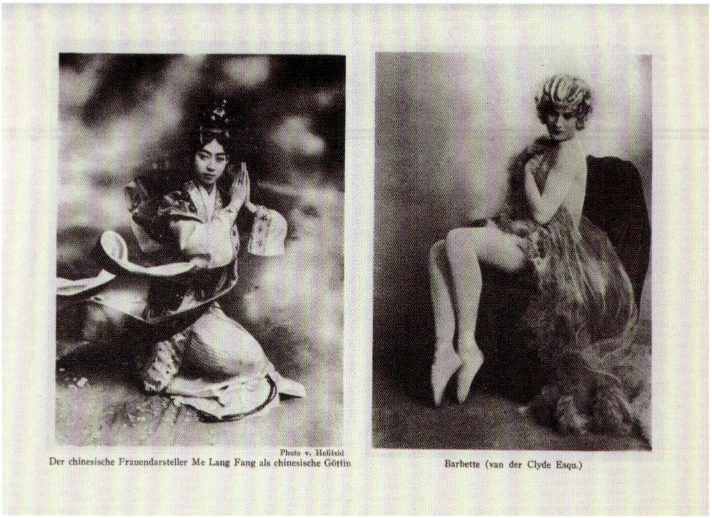

Page from the popular journal *Der Querschnitt* (The Cross Section), vol. 6, no. 12, 1926, p. 967, Tate Archives

example. As a melding of two rival circuses it was able to combine two sets of star attractions for the benefit of their enraptured audiences. Its success established an association between the circus and American popular culture that appeared modern and vital, and proved to have a long legacy. Beckmann was an enthusiastic supporter of this and other circuses, and sought out famous performers, including the great lion tamer Togare, who came to prominence in the 1920s performing with Circus Sarrasani, Circus Carmo and Circus Althoff. Beckmann owned an autographed card from 1927 that shows the shirtless performer in a jewelled belt and headdress. The effect of the costume was to heighten this sense of the exotic, even if Togare was really the stage name of the Hungarian-born Russian Georg Kulovits.[5]

It should be noted that such internationalism was an illusion, to the point of caricature. It presented audiences whose experience and opportunity to travel were very limited (especially in the years of rampant inflation), simultaneously with the exotic 'other' and with the glamour of the United States, obliquely portraying the fruits of its industrialised, capitalist society. The illustrated cultural magazine *Der Querschnitt* (The Cross Section) gives a flavour of such cross-cultural influences. Eclectic in its content, it highlighted and gave a platform to other cultures it deemed exotic and peculiar (including the British). A typical spread would comprise a side-by-side juxtaposition of performers from different parts of the world – such as in a comparison of the cross-dressing actor Me Lang Fang, apparently in traditional Chinese dynastic dress, alongside a photograph of the Texan, Paris-based drag artist, Barbette.[6] It is significant that *Der Querschnitt* was launched in 1921 by Alfred Flechtheim's gallery, which concurrently showed contemporary artists published in the magazine, such as Grosz, Klee and Schlichter. In this way the magazine provided a complex texture of both 'high' and 'low' cultural activities as a reflection of modern life.

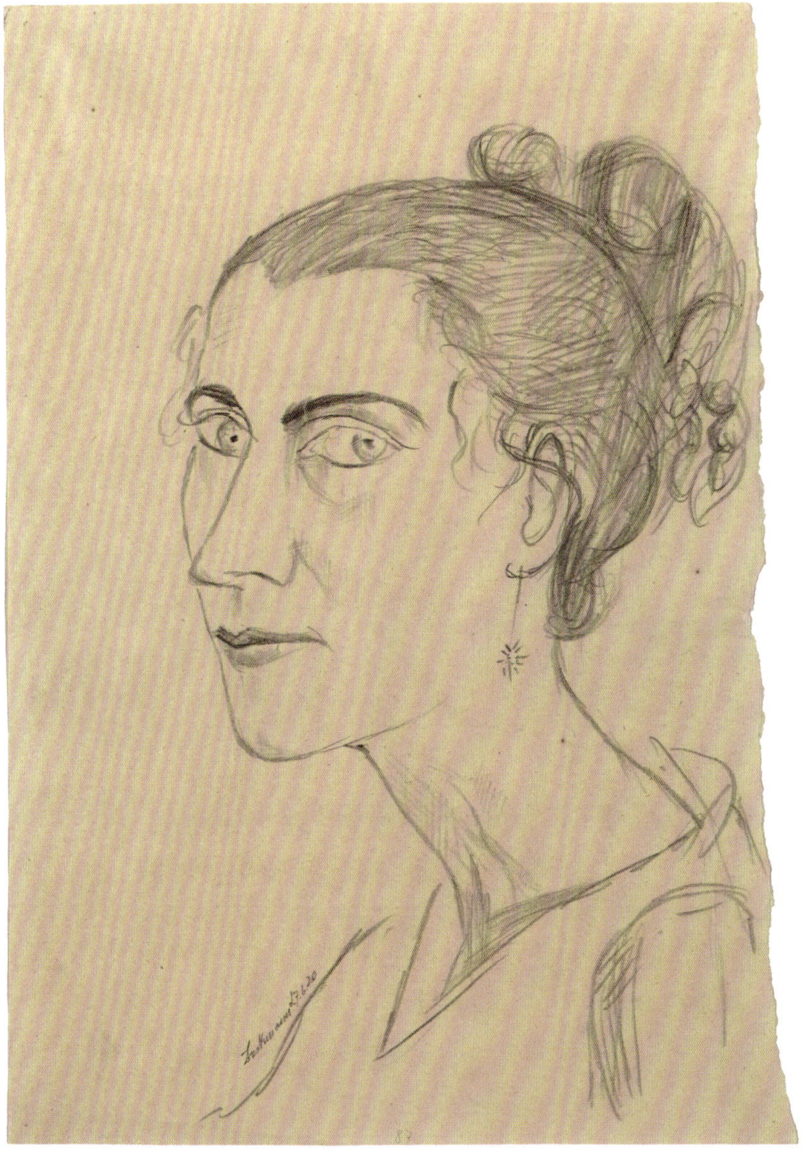

Max Beckmann
Frau Ullstein (Portrait of a Woman)
Frau Ullstein (Porträt einer Frau) 1920
Graphite on paper
33 × 23.8

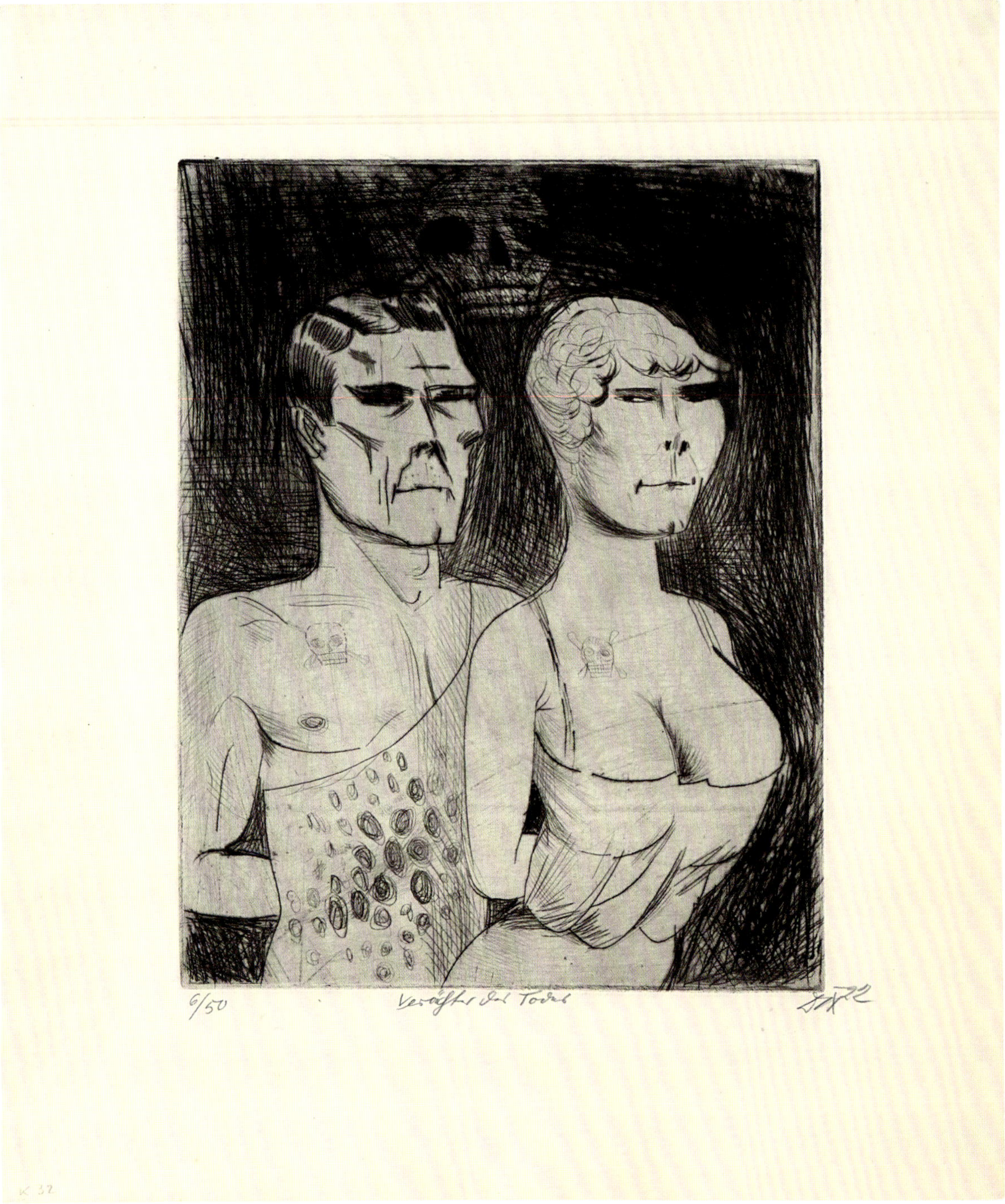
6/50
Verächter des Todes

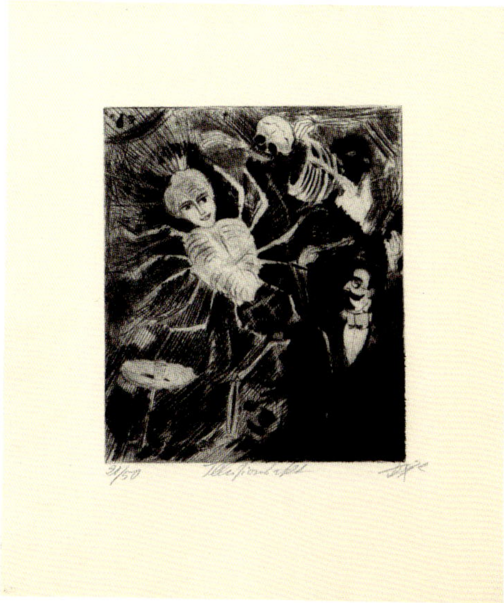

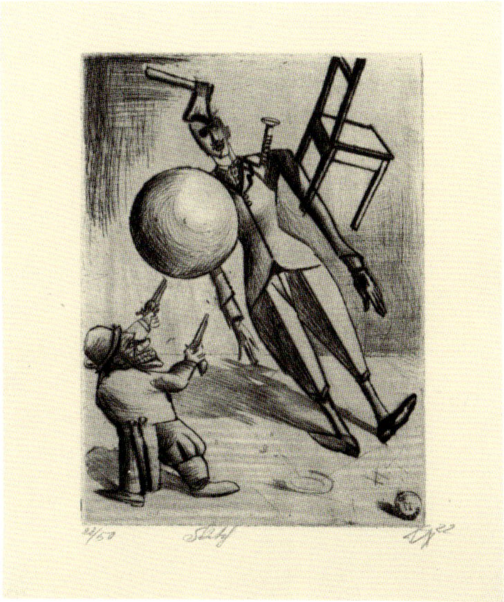

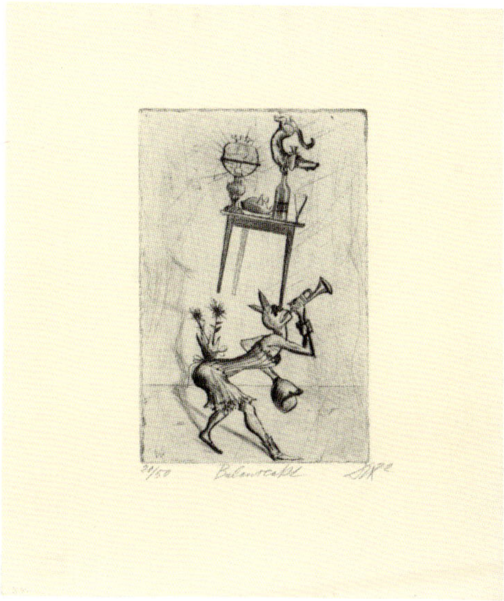

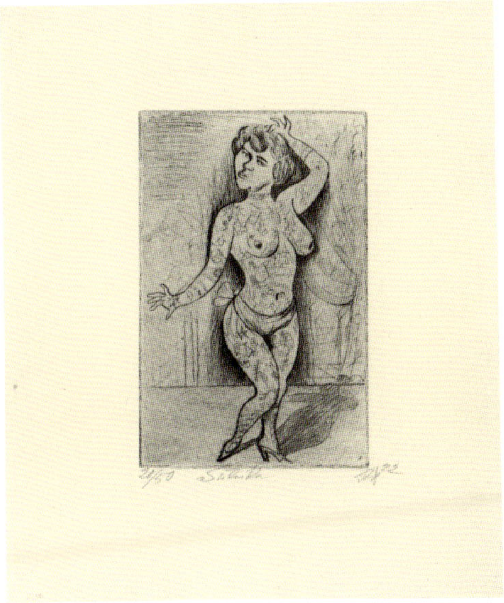

Otto Dix
Zirkus (Circus) 1922
All etching, drypoint on paper
(pp.26–9)

Opposite page:

The Scorners of Death
Die Verächter des Todes 1922
49.7 × 42.8, plate 34.7 × 27.7

This page:

Illusion Act
Illusionsakt
49.5 × 42.9, plate 30 × 25.7
(top left)

Sketch
49.7 × 42.9, plate 39.4 × 29.7
(top right)

Balancing Act
Balanceakt 1922
49.6 × 42.9, plate 29.9 × 19.7
(bottom left)

Maud Arizona (Suleika,
The Tattooed Wonder)
Maud Arizona (Suleika,
das tätowierte Wunder) 1922
49.8 × 42.8, plate 29.9 × 19.8
(bottom right)

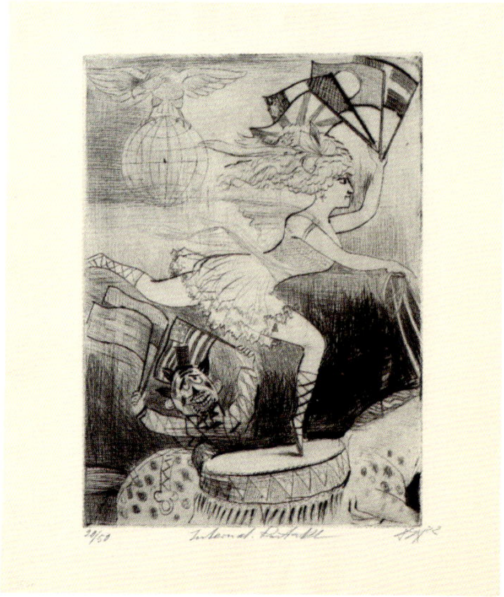

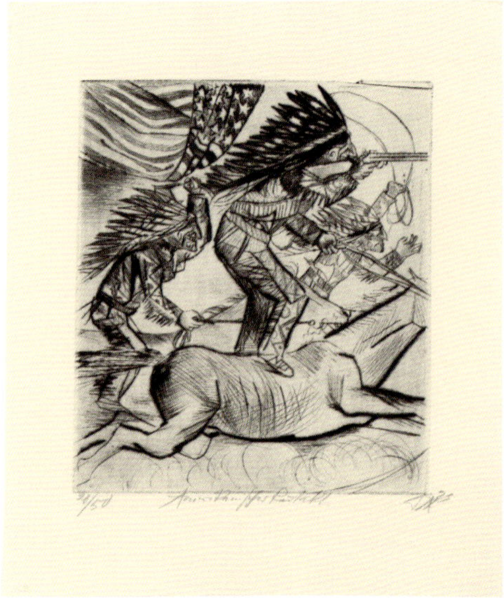

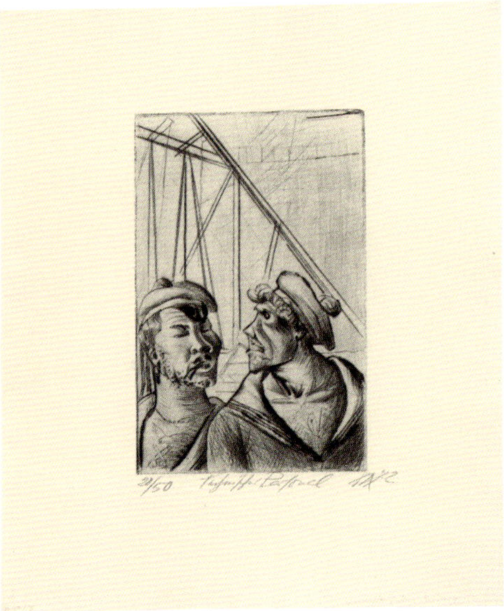

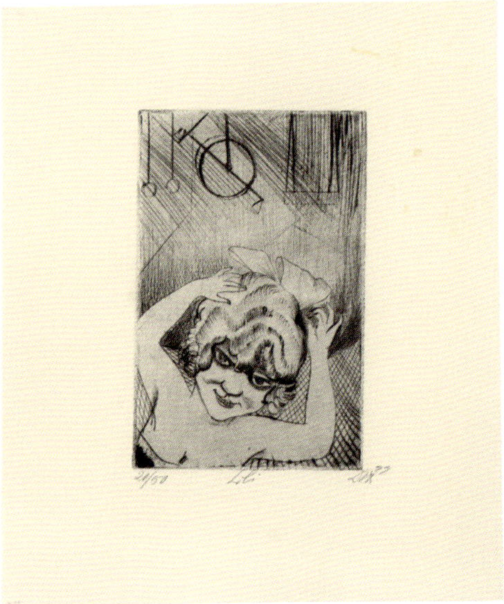

This page:

Otto Dix
International Riding Act
Internationaler Reitakt
49.6 × 43.1, plate 39.9 × 29.8
(top left)

American Riding Act
Amerikanischer Reitakt
49.7 × 42.9, plate 34.7 × 30.9
(top right)

Technical Personnel
Technisches Personal
49.7 × 42.6, plate 30 × 19.8
(bottom left)

Lili, The Queen of the Air
Lili, die Königin der Luft
49.7 × 42.8, plate 29.9 × 19.8
(bottom right)

Opposite page:

Tamer
Dompteuse
49.6 × 42.9, plate 39.9 × 29.7

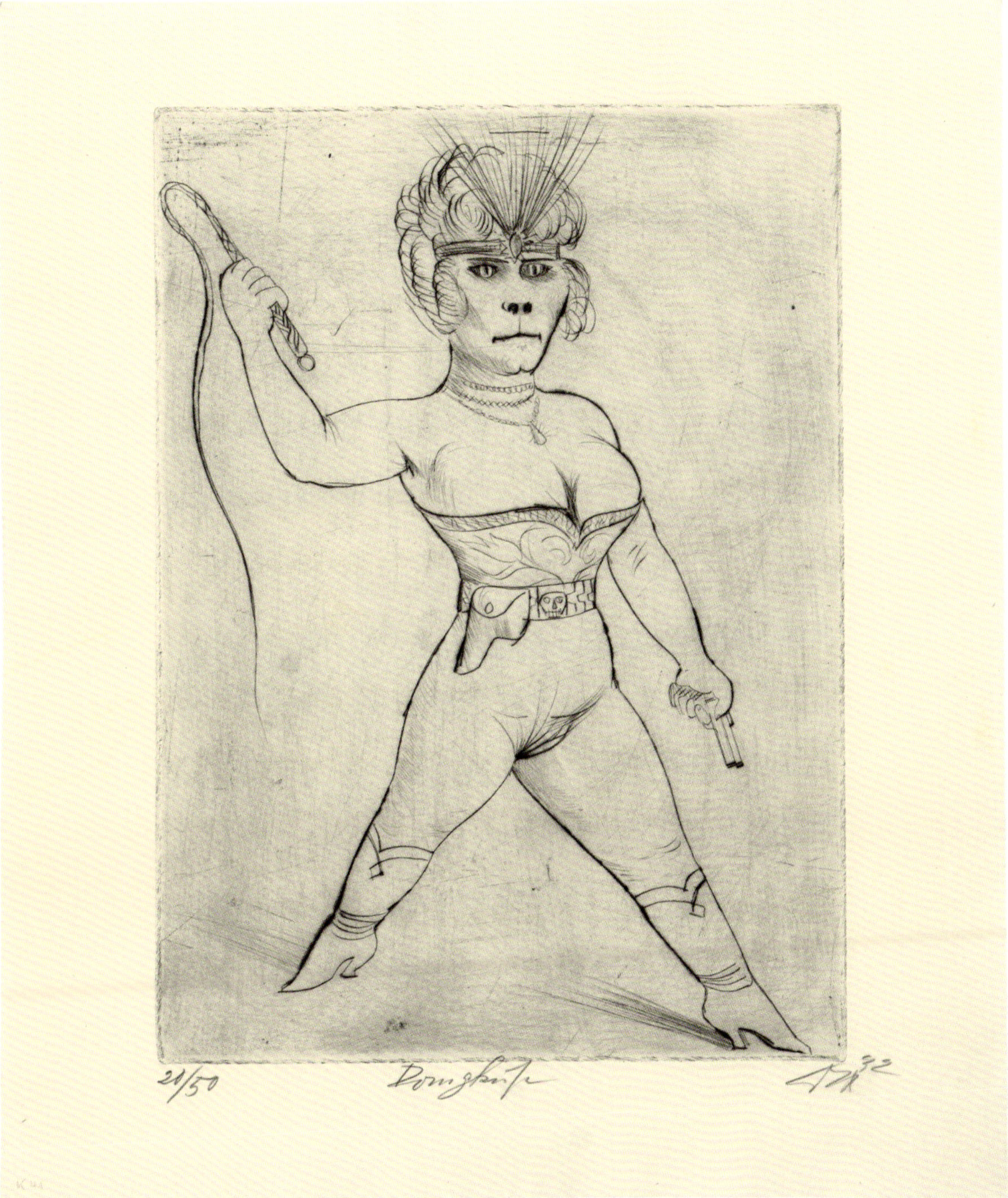
21/50

Within the urban context, the circus was a liminal space: able, on the one hand, to accommodate outsiders, and on the other, to capitalise on this sense of the exotic and the permissive.[7] As a result of this peripheral status there is an obvious difficulty in ascribing national or ethnic identity to the individuals involved. Across photographic depictions, taken either for publicity or documentary purposes (p.31), performers are either unnamed or disguised by their public stage persona that blurs the distinction between reality and fiction. The nomadic nature of the circus and the marginalised status of travelling performers of ethnic groups, who later came under scrutiny and persecution in the Nazi era, has made identifying individuals all the more difficult.[8]

Such conditions set the tone for the portrayals of physical otherness in Dix's portfolio *Zirkus* (Circus). While one of course must account for the idiosyncrasies of Dix's own practice, the peculiarities of depicting supposed family entertainments in such a psychologically dark and transgressive way were shared with his contemporaries. *Circus* was published in 1922 in an edition of fifty by the gallerist Rudolf Nierendorf, who had by September of the same year become the artist's dealer. It consisted of ten prints, each portraying an 'act' as if laying out the programme for an evening's entertainment:

1. *Die Verächter des Todes* (The Scorners of Death)
2. *Illusionsakt* (Illusion Act)
3. *Sketch*
4. *Balanceakt* (Balancing Act)
5. *Maud Arizona* (sometimes credited with the additional title 'Suleika, The Tattooed Wonder')
6. *Internationaler Reitakt* (International Riding Act)
7. *Amerikanischer Reitakt* (American Riding Act)
8. *Technisches Personal* (Technical Personnel)
9. *Lili, der Königin der Luft* (Lili, The Queen of the Air)
10. *Dompteuse* (Tamer)

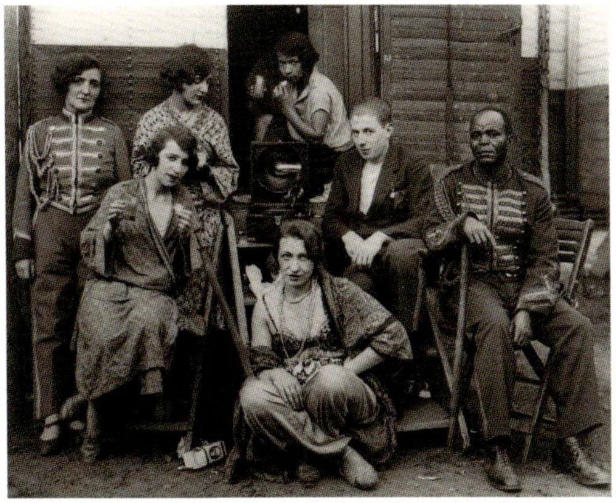

August Sander
Circus Artistes 1926–32
Gelatin silver print on paper, 23.4 x 29.2
Die Photographische Sammlung/
SK Stiftung Kultur – August Sander Archive, Cologne

Notable in the early images is a combination of danger and mystery. The couple parading in *The Scorners of Death* (p.26) display thinly clad bodies and a fixed determination. They stand, literally, in the face of death (the skull in the background), which is defied in their high-wire or trapeze performances. That mortal danger could be offered up as mass entertainment with the memory of war still fresh (as Dix's *War* portfolio demonstrated), captures the paradoxical atmosphere of Weimar culture.[9] The dark humour of this postwar escapism also appears in the childlike threat and accomplishment of *Illusion Act* and *Balancing Act* (p.27).

If the early prints serve as the warm-up acts, the main events are striking for their combination of daring located in relation to American culture. *Maud Arizona*, also known as 'Suleika, The Tattooed Wonder' (p.27), is a character who, given her multiple and varying names, is of uncertain nationality. Through her presentation as a social oddity, she is but one of a number of 'tattooed wonders' who gained popularity at that time, being showcased in port cities of the era.[10] Dix portrays her in a performative mode, assuming a *contrapposto* stance akin to classical sculpture. Given his keen eye for accentuating his subjects' physical traits, it is surprising that Maud's tattoos are barely discernible. For Dix, they are an embellishment rather than a defining feature, a possibility that is confirmed when viewed alongside the drawing *Die Schöne Mally!* (Beautiful Mally!) 1920, which shows a woman of virtually the same proportions and a similar pose.

The most explicit examples of the circus's international outlook come in the two riding act prints. *International Riding Act* (p.28) shows a blonde, balletic woman accomplishing the daredevil feat of balancing on one leg on a horse in motion. Her posture is made all the more perilous as she is carrying a number of flags representing

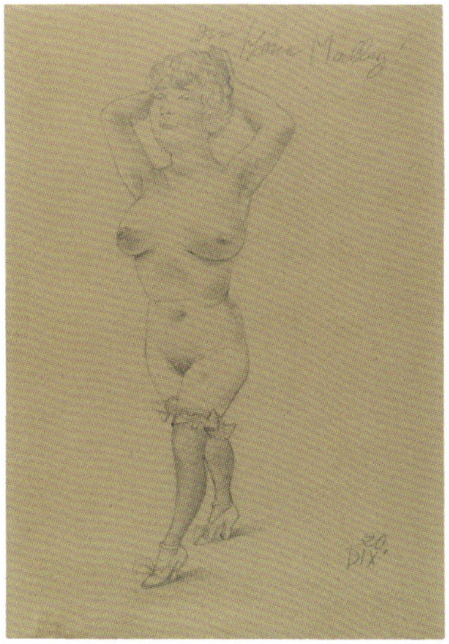

Otto Dix
Beautiful Mally!
Die Schöne Mally! 1920
Pencil on paper
42.2 × 30.2
Museum of Modern Art, New York
John S. Newberry Fund [464.1967]

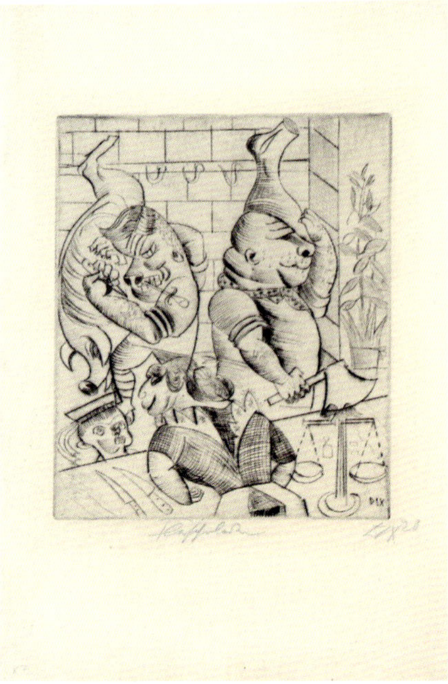

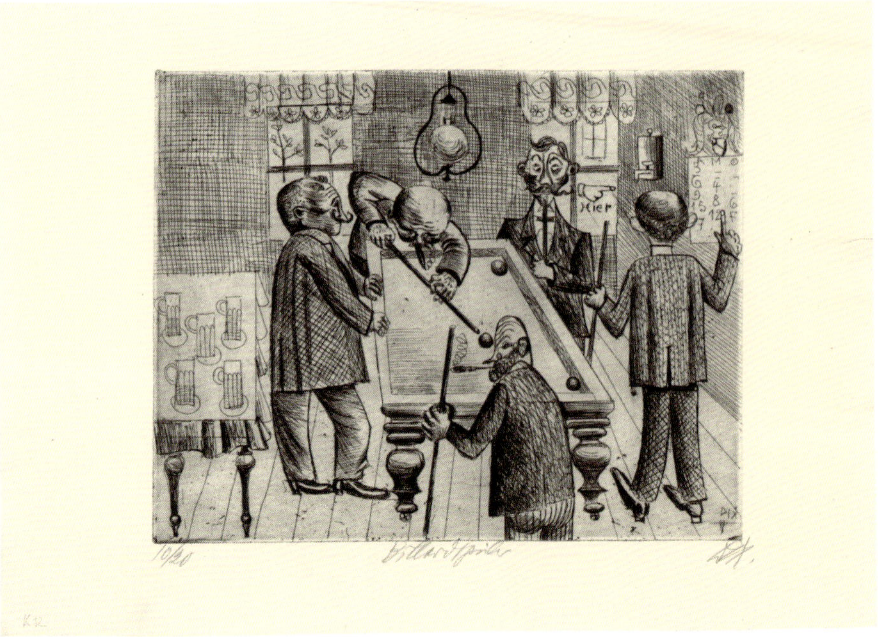

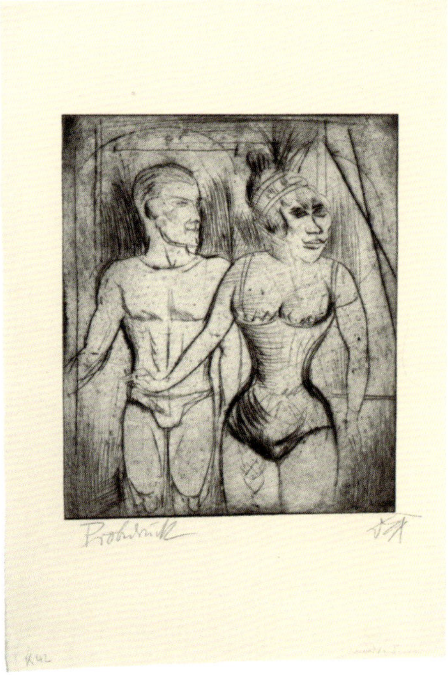

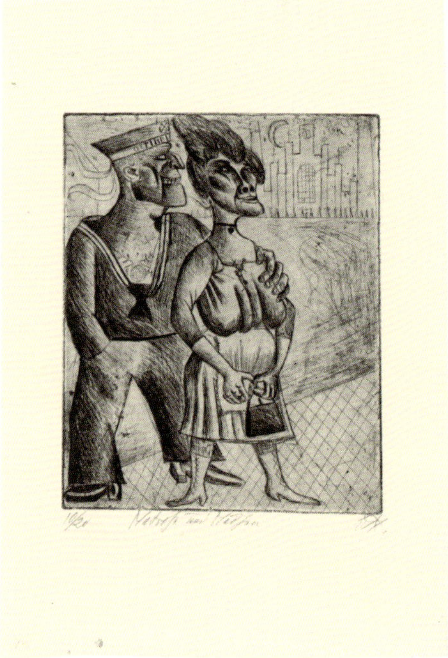

This page, clockwise from top left:

Otto Dix
Butcher Shop
Fleischerladen 1920
Etching, drypoint on paper
49.5 × 33.8, plate 29.5 × 25.8

Billiard Players
Billiardspieler 1920
Etching, drypoint on paper
34 × 48.8, plate 22.5 × 33.3

Sailor and Girl
Matrose und Mädchen 1920
Etching, drypoint on paper
48.7 × 34.2, plate 30 × 24.8

Performers
Artisten 1922
Etching, drypoint on paper
49.2 × 34, plate 29.9 × 25.8

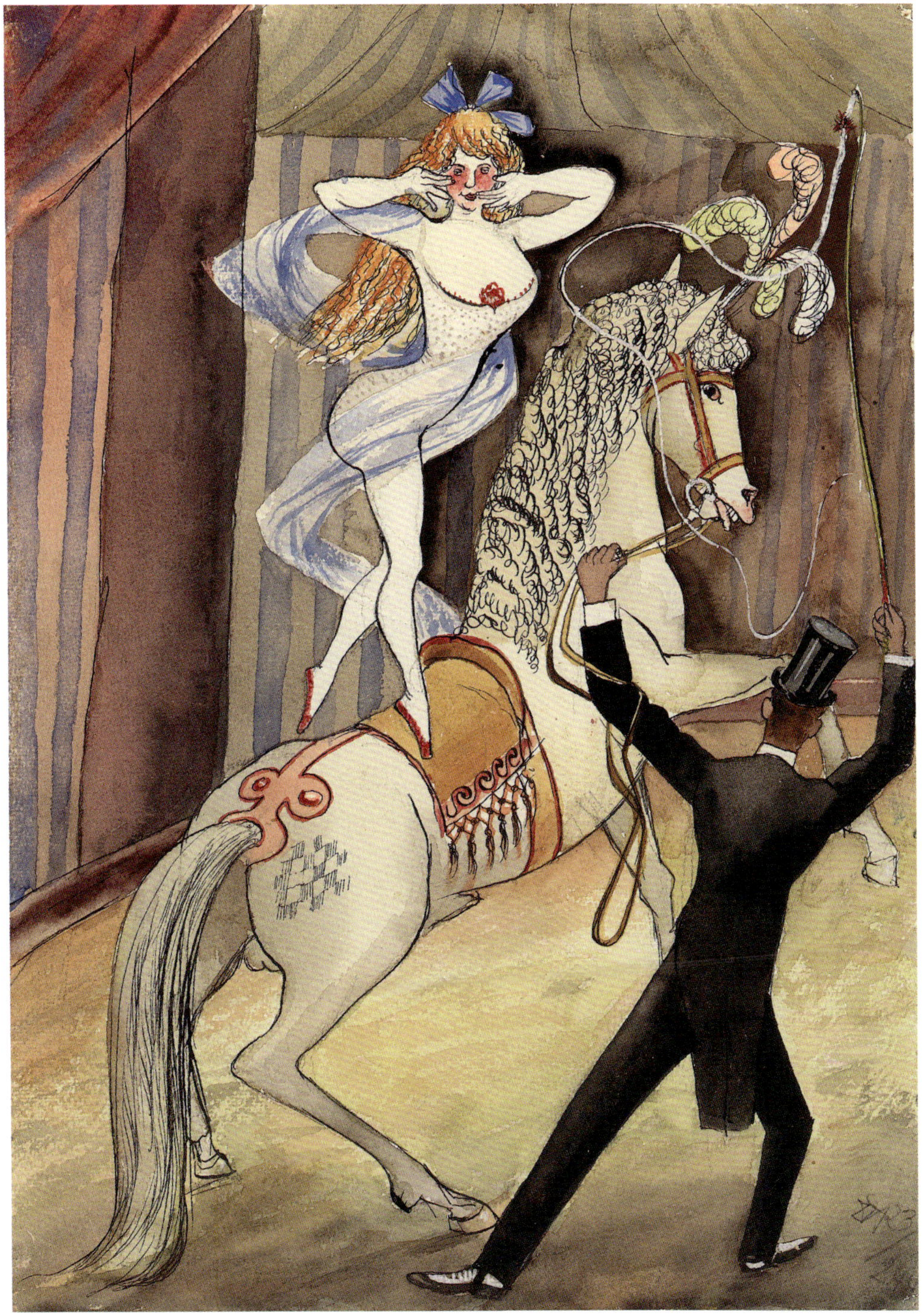

Otto Dix
Circus Scene (Riding Act)
Zirkusszene (Reitakt) 1923
Watercolour, pen
and ink on paper
38.1 × 27.6

different nations. Grimacing up at her is a figure also bearing flags, including the stars and stripes of the United States. In the background is the floating apparition of a globe mounted by an eagle: the symbol of the US Marine Corps. Complementing this is a second, more precarious representation of American culture: titled *American Riding Act* (p.28), the composition portrays a figure adorned in a feathered headdress and fringed garments who stands atop a bareback horse, its legs suspended in mid-air as it courses around the circus ring at exhilarating speed. That the face is contorted, and painted with swirls and whorls, serves to heighten this sense of physical and (implied) ethnic difference.

The degree to which US-European influence travelled in both directions is further encapsulated in the subject of the penultimate print. Lilian Leitzel, a German aerial performer of Hungarian and Czech origin who eventually moved to California, was a star of the Ringling Brothers and Barnum & Bailey Circus. Purported to be a *prima donna assoluta* of the circus world, Dix emphasises her childlike appearance, thereby highlighting the ways in which she contravened normative social codes of adulthood (p.28).

Dix's final print is the portrayal of an unnamed *Dompteuse* or 'tamer' (p.29), and a fitting image with which to sign off in its intrigue and peculiarity. If isolated from the *Circus* prints, the Tamer is unavoidably identifiable as a dominatrix, redolent with erotic power, not only through the whip and pistol that she brandishes, but also through a restrictive corset that strains and articulates her genital area. For these details alone the image appears transgressive. Glowing eyes, her muzzle-like mouth and the shoes that resemble hooves suggest that the character has morphed into the very animal that defines her role, recalling Dix's comment about humanity's innate bestial nature. These physical attributes instil her with an ambiguity, it not being clear as to whether she is an entertainer of children or of adults. This apparent deviance may be why the image was later singled out for reproduction in the pamphlet for the Nazis' anti-modernist *Entartete Kunst* exhibition of so-called 'degenerate art'.

If violence and eroticism pervade the *Circus* series, the question must be asked how this concurs with works relating to the theme of *lustmord* or 'sex murder', a recurring subject across Dix's practice in painting, drawing and printing. It is discernible that, for Dix and his contemporaries, there was little distinction between the overtones of these

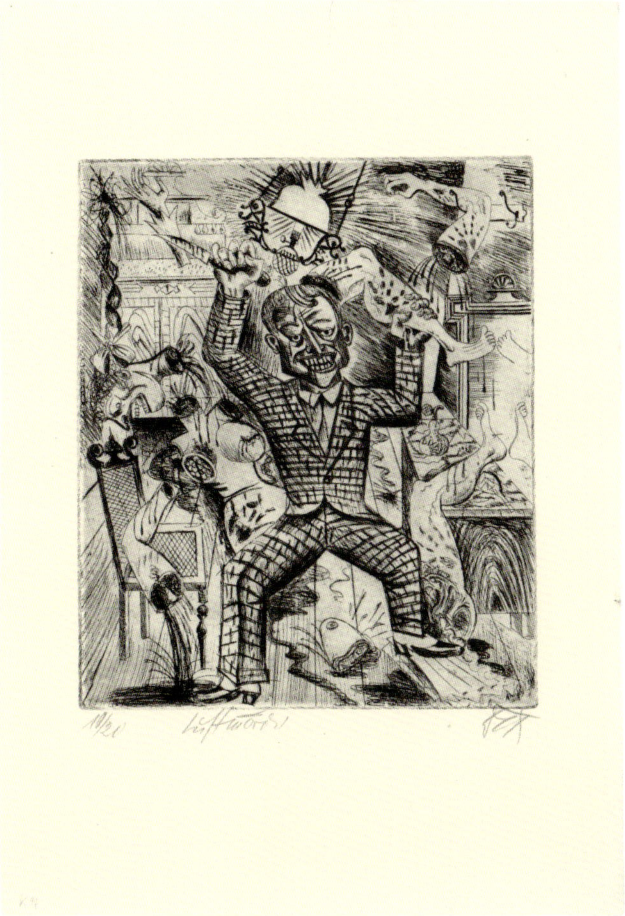

Otto Dix
Lust Murderer
Lustmörder 1920
Etching on paper
49 × 34.1
plate 30 × 25.7

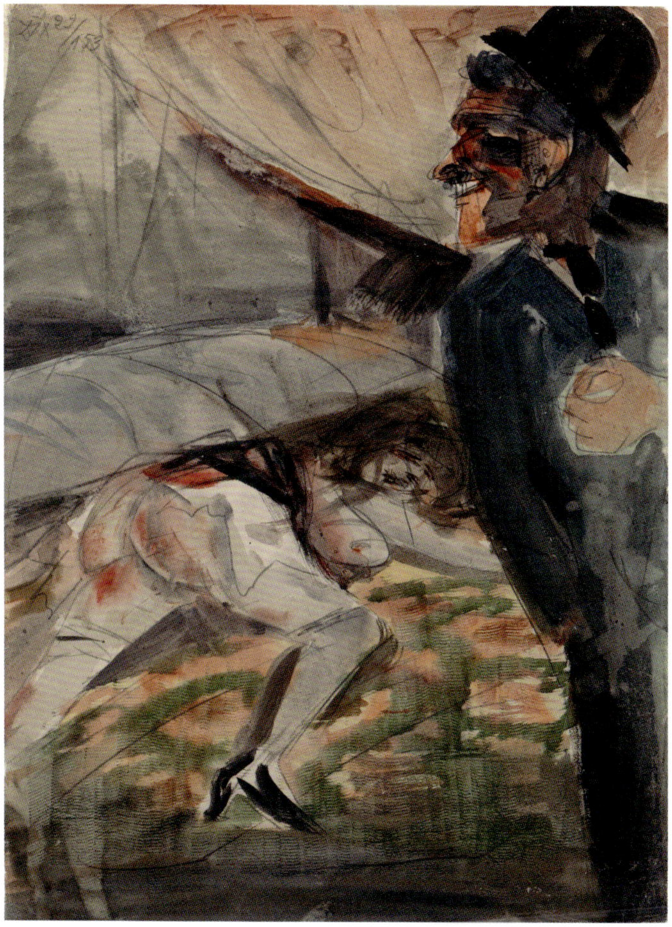

Otto Dix
Lust Murder
Lustmord 1922
Watercolour, ink and
graphite on paper
48.5 × 36.5

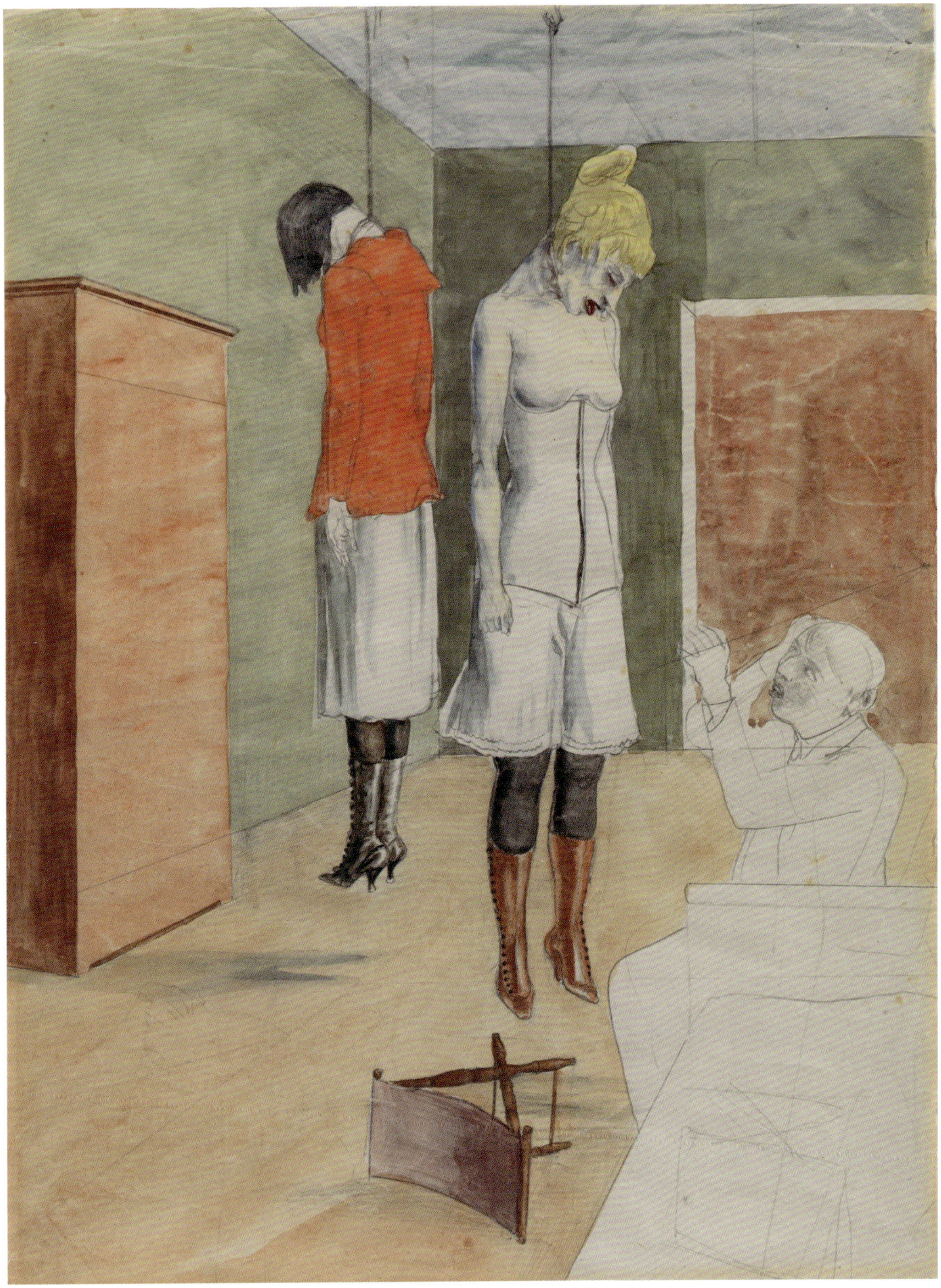

Rudolf Schlichter
The Artist with Two Hanged Women
Der Künstler mit zwei erhängten Frauen 1924
Watercolour and graphite on paper
45.3 × 34

genres. The theme of the sexually motivated killing of women featured strongly in the art and literature of the Weimar period, despite having precedents across Europe: for example in Oskar Kokoschka's 1909 expressionist play *Mörder, Hoffnung de Frauen* (Murder, Hope of Women) and Émile Zola's 1890 novel *La Bête Humaine* (The Beast Within). The subject, which was exclusively the preserve of male artists, appears repeatedly, even to the point of betraying an apparent sympathy with the role of the murderer. This would seem to be the case in the alarming imagery of Schlichter's watercolour *Der Künstler mit zwei erhängten Frauen* (The Artist with Two Hanged Women) 1924 (p.36). Although the man seems horrified by his discovery, there is an undertow of fetishism that links to other works by the artist and his own documentation of sexual fantasies.[11] In Grosz's poem 'Berlin 1917', which echoes some of the imagery in his painting *Selbstmörder* (Suicide) 1916 (p.17), a sinister atmosphere of crime is also evoked:

> Gloomily the overcoat flaps at the pimp's bones,
> Back bent, brass knuckles fixed,
> Descending with a sharp Solingen knife
> Deep into tenements
> Into fur shop and silk houses
> Or coal cellars
> Afterwards one sometimes finds a bloody
> Piece of taffeta or a wool stocking
> Or the bill with a handprint.[12]

In his paintings and drawings Grosz depicted himself in multiple roles within images that engage with sexual violence and which reveal a paranoid experience of reality that may be taken as symptomatic of wider Weimar anxieties.[13] The poet and critic Theodor Däubler, who was lionised in Heinrich Maria Davringhausen's 1917 portrait (p.11), was responsible for the earliest review of Grosz's work in 1916, in which he identified the artist's predilection for depicting private scenes of urban life as if framed by a window, thereby rendering the viewer complicit in this fictive voyeurism.[14]

A further example of self-identification is found in Dix's print *Lustmörder* (Lust Murderer) 1920 (p.35), in which the artist's name is inscribed within the composition (on the table, next to the dismembered leg). Surviving photographs of a lost painting of the same name show that Dix had applied a handprint directly onto the surface of the canvas, lending a further physical identification to the work.[15]

It has been suggested that the *Circus* series offered a form of mental respite for Dix. Tellingly, his most famous print cycle, *The War*, was created afterwards, between 1923 and 1924. Of his experience, Dix had remarked: 'However hideously savage war may be, with lice, mud, all those insane noises ... I could not possibly miss it. You have to see man in his unbridled state in order to know something about him.'[16]

In an urban metropolis, reeling from the postwar moment, it is troubling but not entirely beyond belief that this shift in the moral structure of society and the combination of violence and permissiveness would find form in artistic expression. The increasing emancipation for women from domestic life and the institutionalisation of brothels in military encampments, which Dix notoriously frequented, is also considered to have contributed to visualisations of violence against women. Furthermore, the advent of mass entertainments, the rise of the urban metropolis and its 'dangers', and the sense of a world beyond Germany's borders – particularly in the realm of art – all worked in tandem. It could be argued that the apparent transgression of convention, whether it be sexual or violent, was a reaction to the changes that the new urban and social reality had facilitated. It may be seen as a form of catharsis or an 'acting out' in circumstances that were often sinister, often unreal.

KW

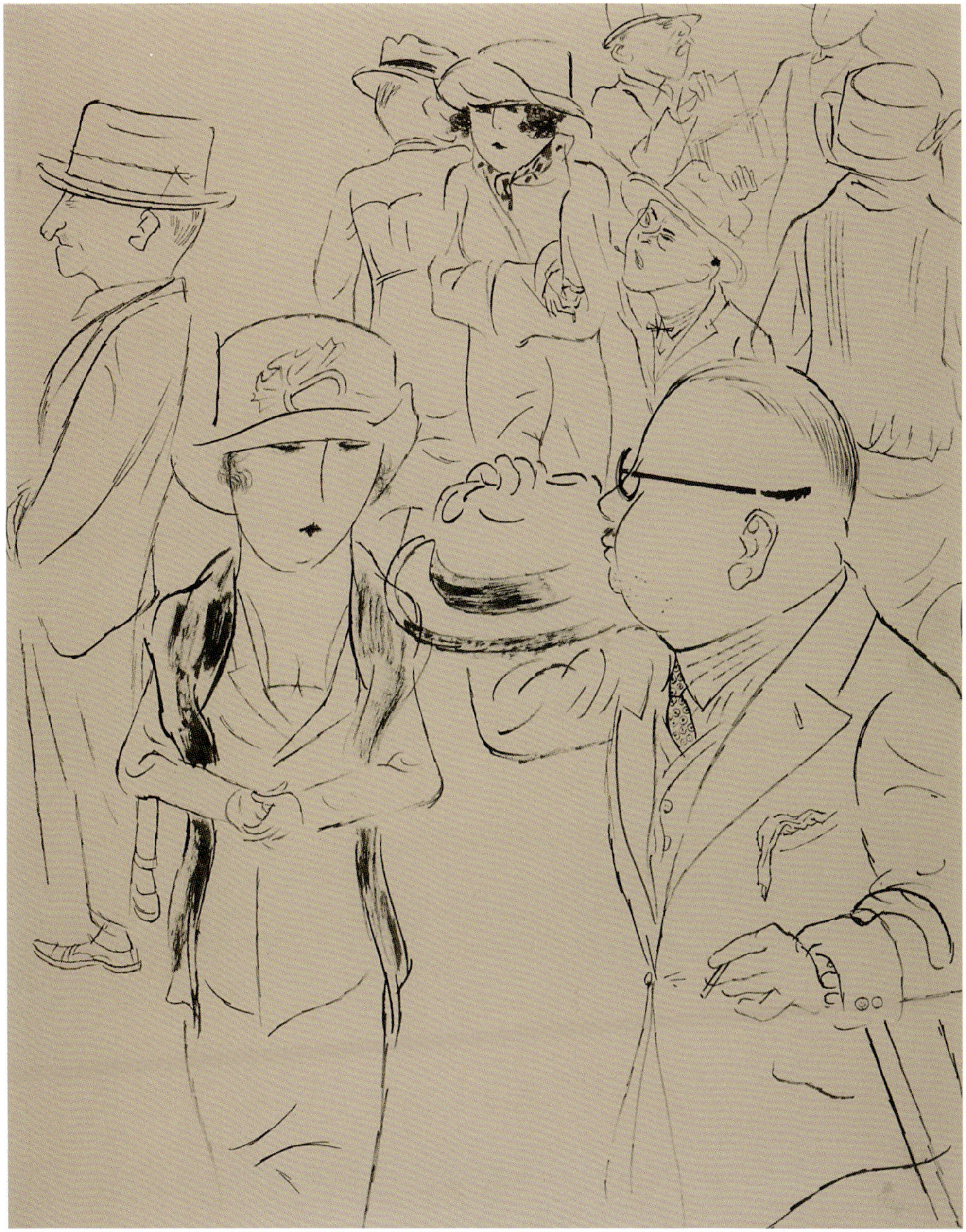

George Grosz
Drawing for 'The Mirror of the Bourgeoisie'
Drawing for 'Der Spiesser-Spiegel' c.1925
Ink on paper
62.9 × 50.5

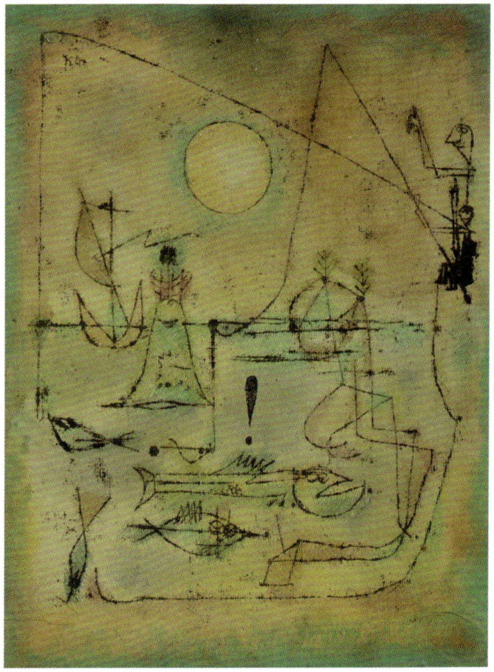

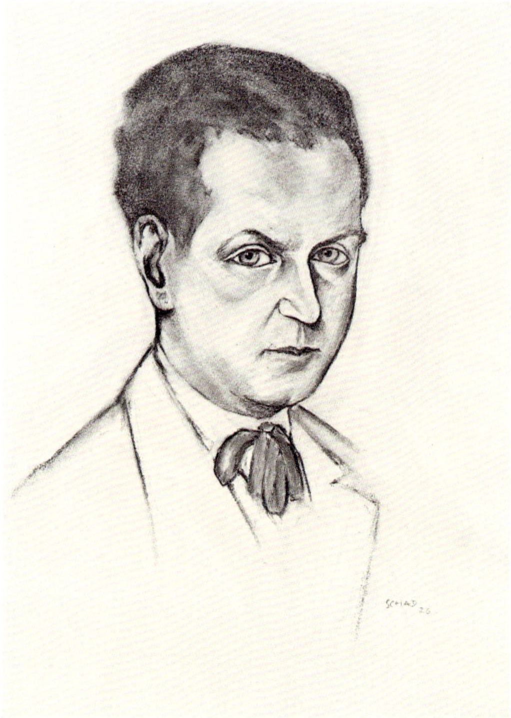

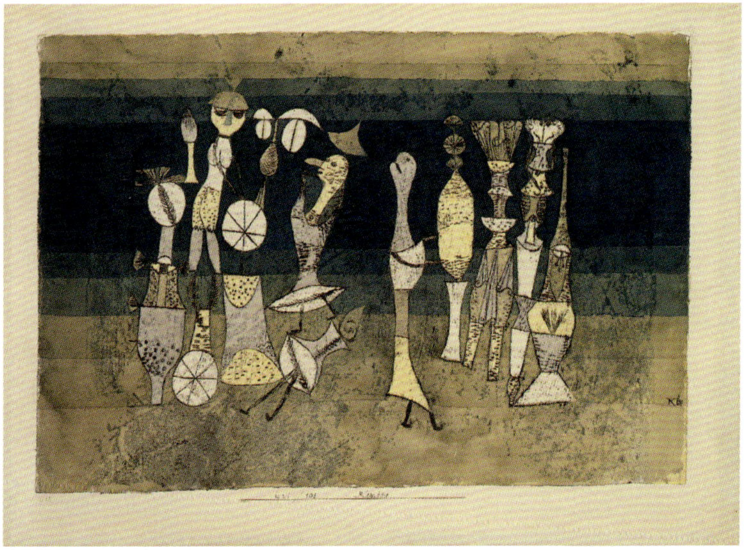

Paul Klee
They're Biting
Sie beissen an 1920
Watercolour and oil paint on paper
31.1 × 23.5 (top left)

Christian Schad
Prof. Holzmeister 1926
Charcoal on paper
54.2 × 40 (top right)

Paul Klee
Comedy
Komödie 1921
Watercolour and oil paint on paper
30.5 × 45.4 (left)

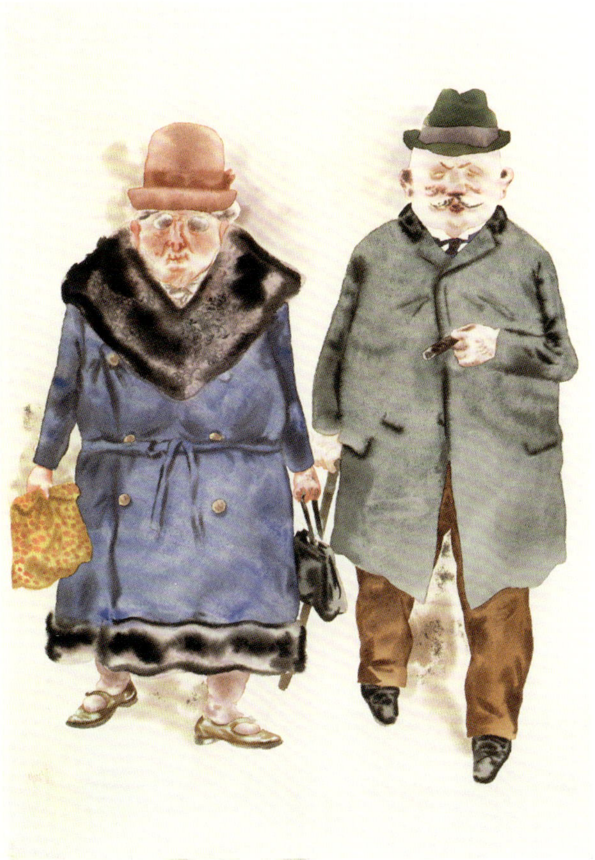

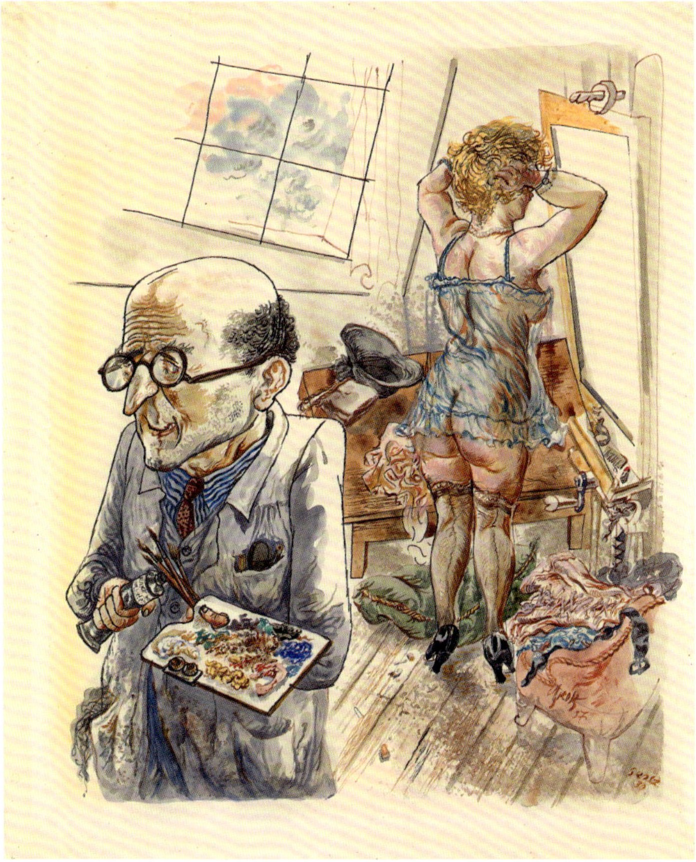

George Grosz
A Married Couple
Ehepaar 1930
Watercolour on paper
66 × 47.3

George Grosz
Self-Portrait with Model in the Studio
Selbstbildnis mit Modell im Atelier 1930–7
Watercolour, gouache, pen and ink on paper
50.5 × 44

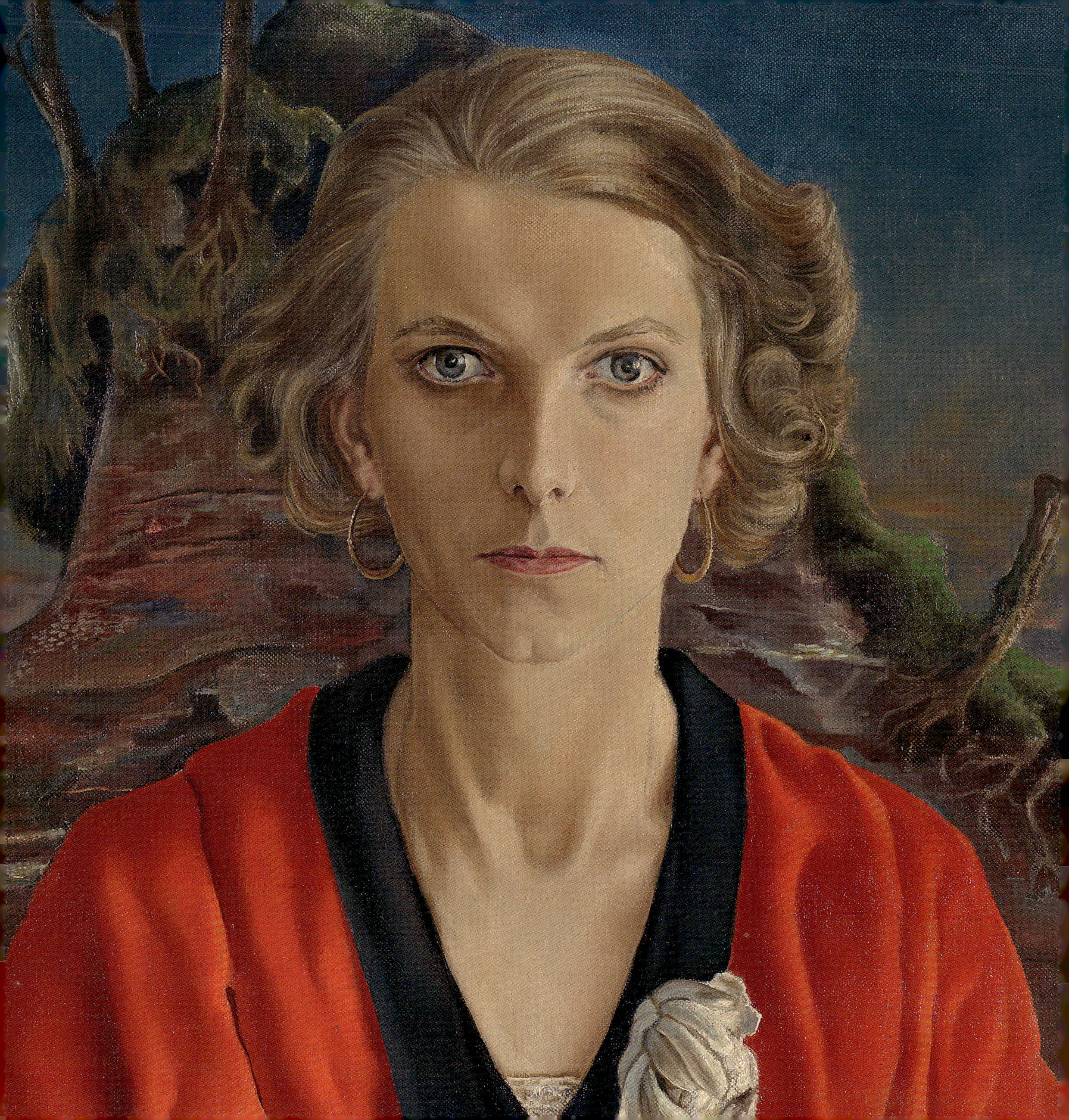

From the Street to the Studio: 'Pleasurable Abundance'

In March 1926, the artist Werner Gräff offered an optimistic view of the enriched texture of modern life in an article entitled 'Pleasurable Abundance – by Means of New Technology'. Published in the constructivist periodical *G*, he counted off a range of contemporary pastimes:

> Amusement park, pleasure flying, jazz band, elegance, Chaplin, and snow-shoeing – in addition, world travel now and then, and, if need be, spas – all this for everyone, and on demand, is no less important than clean streets and spacious, salutary dwellings. And all this with a two- or four-hour work-day; it is achieved through a complete instrumental organisation of the earth.[1]

Through such enthusiasms, Gräff captured a sense of the faith that could be placed in technology in the mid-1920s. Innovation and industrialisation could hold out the promise of relief from drudgery (even if mechanisation could ultimately carry the threat of a return to mass unemployment). This positive view seemed to be confirmed by the pace of urban life, by newspapers and advertising, and by the wider availability of the commodities of the 'machine age': cameras, radios and telephones, cinemas and motor cars, vacuum cleaners and underground railways (together with developments that have now all but passed into history: gramophones, the telegraph, ocean liners and airships). All were part of an irresistible and exponential technological progress popularly associated with Americanisation through the fabled achievements of production-line capitalism embodied by Ford cars and Hollywood entertainments. This was modernity: the sleek, mass-produced, hygienic modernity of which the qualities of magic realism – cool, smooth, polished – were a part. Some were sceptical of American influence and what the author Stefan Zweig termed the 'monotonisation of the world'.[2] It is a measure of those who regarded it with optimism that Gräff could recommend the regimentation that would accompany this, still impending, technological revolution as requiring 'the elemental restructuring of all of life with an aim toward clarity – order – extreme economy.'[3] As much as the trans-Atlantic example, he may have been looking east to the Five Year Plan of Soviet industrialisation as a point of reference.

Detail, see p.67

Yesterday I used a radio receiver for the first time. This was an agreeable way, I found, to be convinced that entertainment is available. You hear something that is far away, and the people producing these audible sounds are speaking, as it were, to everyone – in other words – they are completely ignorant as to the number and characteristics of their listeners ... When a group of people listens to the radio, they naturally stop carrying on conversations. While they are occupied with listening, the art of companionship is, as it were, neglected a little. This is a quite proper, obvious consequence. I and the people sitting beside me heard a cello being played in England. There was something strange and marvellous about this.

Robert Walser, 'Radio', May–June 1926, in *Microscripts*, translated by Susan Bernofsky, New York 2010, p.23

As part of the reconstruction of the Weimar period, the cities were sites for new housing and magnets for the rural population. Berlin had two million inhabitants in 1910 but, despite the wartime losses, this had doubled by 1920.[4] Continuing (and adapting) industrialisation demanded workers, and there was potential for casual employment that in the rural areas was inevitably seasonal. Flexibility generated innovation, as exemplified by Walter Gropius's desire to reconcile art, craft and industry through the teaching and commercialisation of design at the Bauhaus.[5] This was the period of extraordinary exhibitions that shaped new media, from the Bauhaus exhibition itself in 1923, to the International Press exhibition in Cologne in 1928 and *Film und Foto* in Stuttgart the following year.[6] This was also the moment of a cinematic reflection and invention of the new city, from the flawed vision of the future in Fritz Lang's *Metropolis* 1927, starring the robotised Brigitte Helm, to the seduction available in the cabarets captured in Josef von Sternberg's *Der Blaue Engel* (The Blue Angel) 1930 starring Marlene Dietrich.

Artists engaged with realist practices captured all manner of urban existence as they sought both to gauge contemporary life and to reflect it back in such a way as to make a living. A number of Communist artists, including the Cologne Progressives who emerged from dada circles in the city, focused on campaigning subject matter often distributed through printmaking. An early example, emerging in the chaotic aftermath of war, was the collective portfolio that Angelika and Heinrich Hoerle, Franz Seiwert and others made to commemorate the Communist leaders Rosa Luxemburg and Karl Liebknecht, who were murdered by right-wing paramilitaries in 1919. Such apparently Soviet-inspired activities were viewed with official suspicion during the continuing Allied occupation of the Rhineland.

Urban experience differed considerably. The devastating toll of the war was human rather than structural, as the physical destruction had been concentrated beyond German borders: from the Marne and the Somme, to the Piave and the Pripet Marshes. This meant that in some places artists found views that transcended the immediate past and conveyed continuity rather than rupture. As an artist within Franz Roh's circle in Munich, Alexander Kanoldt was most in sympathy with the Italian metaphysical painters' vision of permanence that alluded to Quattrocento precedents (p.61). By contrast, Albert Birkle's view of Passau in 1925 emphasises the historic texture with a

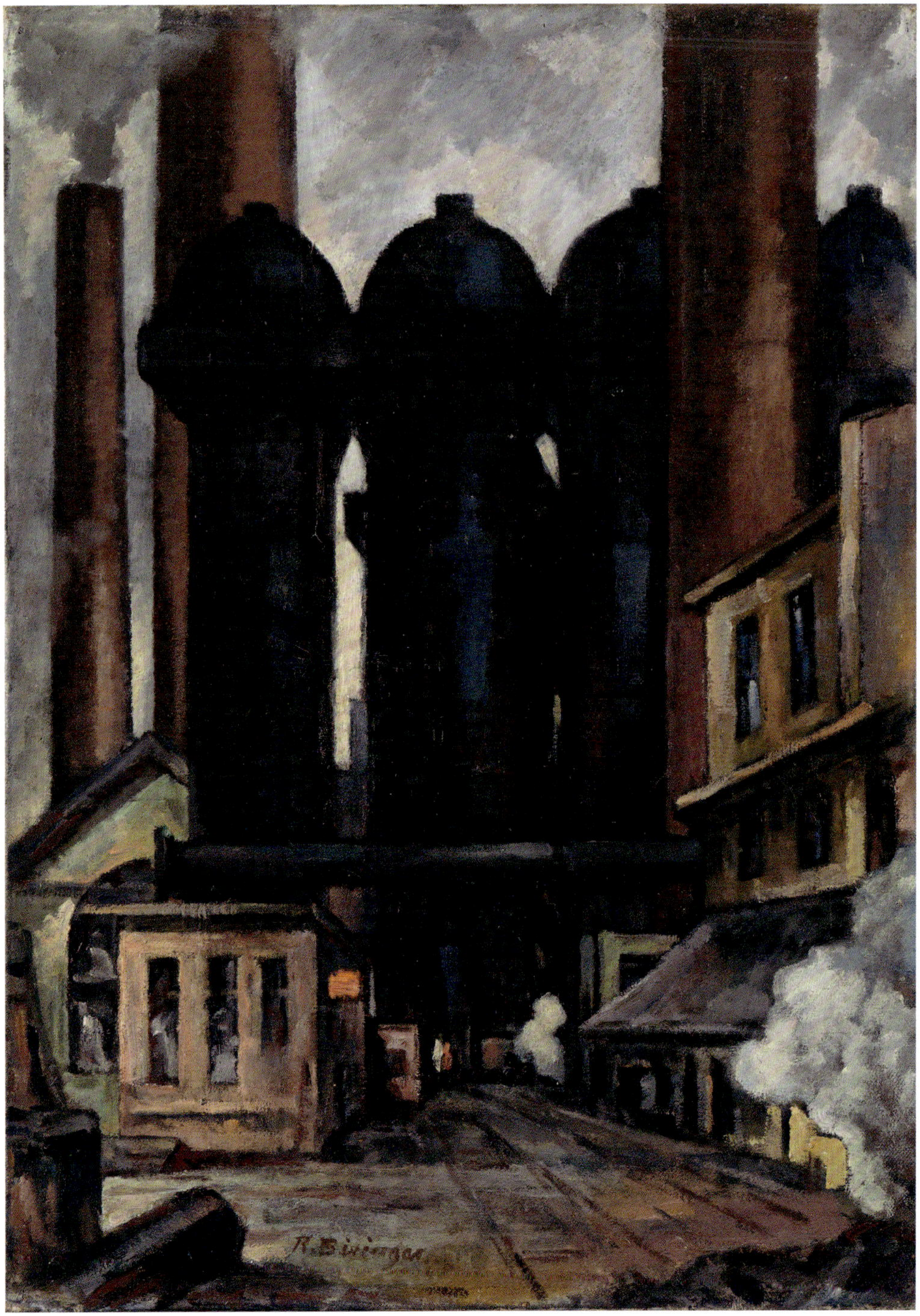

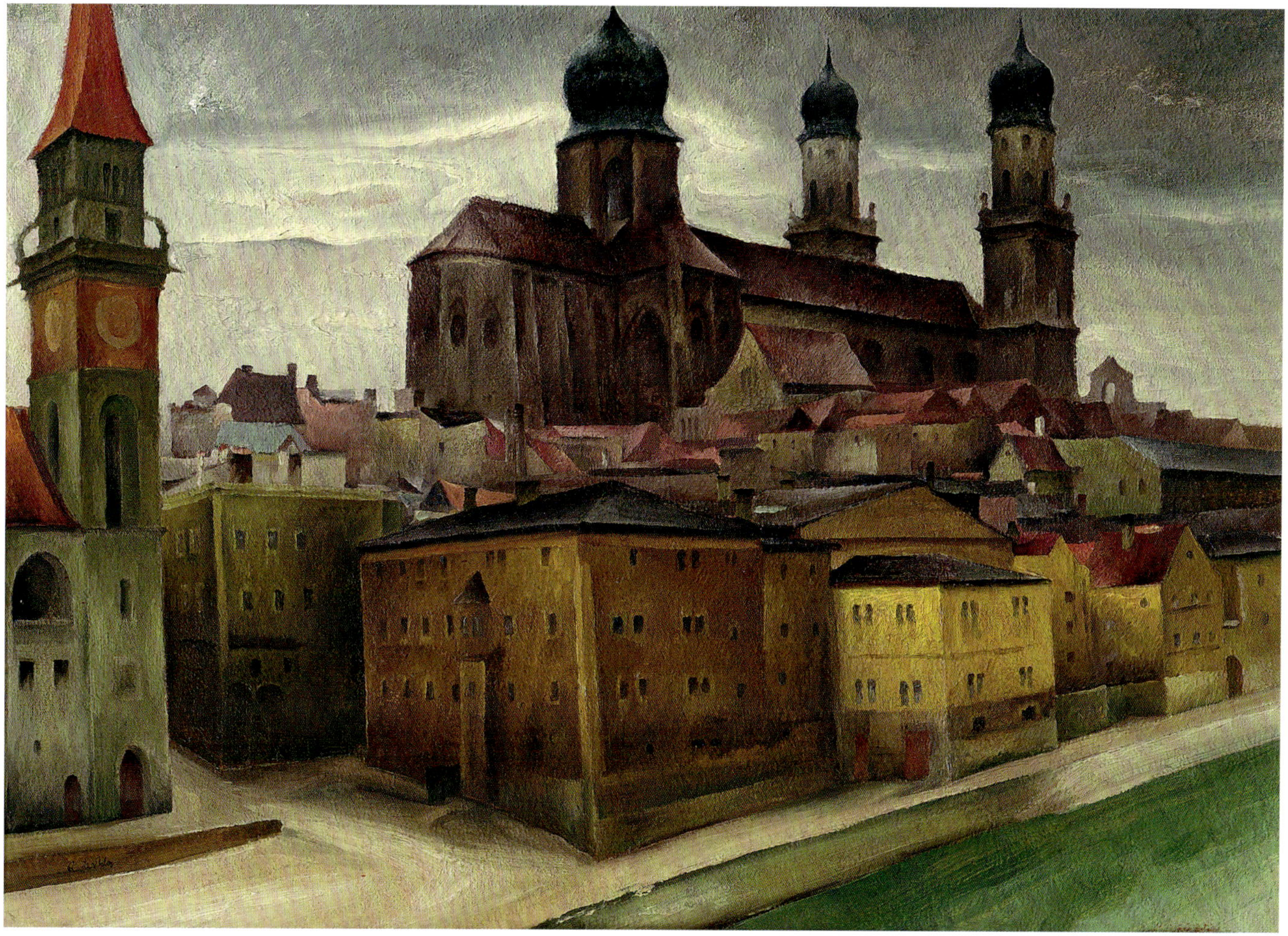

Richard Biringer
Krupp Works, Engers am Rhein
Krupp-Werke, Engers am Rhein 1925
Oil paint on canvas
67.5 × 49.5
(left)

Albert Birkle
Passau 1925
Oil paint on hardboard
51 × 71
(above)

recognisable portrayal of the city's Cathedral of St Stephen on a promontory above the Danube (p.47). This seems to suggest the persistence of the Baroque civilisation of central Europe over recent events, even if the atmospheric sky may indicate troubles embedded in this tradition.

In other cities the historic texture was giving way to ad hoc development. The bourgeois pastimes that Gräff enumerated emerged side by side with the transport infrastructure, manufacturing and heavy industry that sustained them. The railway arches that vaulted through suburb and centre alike, aligned with ports (p.49) and power stations, factories and depots. The results, which were hardly unproblematic, were traced in photographs and films. Notable among the latter was Walter Ruttmann's *Berlin: Die Sinfonie der Großstadt* (Berlin, Symphony of a Great City 1927), which gave rise to a critical debate about the city's development and provoked Siegfried Kracauer to compare the Kurfürstendamm (seen in the film) to a film set and to describe it as 'the embodiment of an empty-flowing time in which nothing is allowed to last'.[7]

The results of the new urbanisation were also traceable, more modestly, in paintings such as Richard Biringer's 1925 image of the Krupp works closing out the sky in Engers am Rhein (p.46). Beyond this sense of industrial dominance over the local population, the painting indirectly addresses the contentious subject of the industrialists who had fed the war machine and then had, through diversification, weathered the disarmament demanded at the Armistice. Their success helped to stabilise the economy but was bound up in the popular imagination with the cause and the neglect of those abandoned on the streets. In 1923, however, such factories were briefly a rallying point in response to the renewed occupation by French and Belgian troops (the same event that delayed Hartlaub's *Neue Sachlichkeit* exhibition in Mannheim). Outrage at this action lead to a financially disastrous general strike that briefly bound together a fragmented society against its common enemy. Such solidarity was short-lived, and the industrialists once more became targets. George Grosz wrote in 1924, 'Today I no longer hate people indiscriminately; today I hate their bad institutions and those in power who defend these institutions.'[8] More directly, John Heartfield began to revolutionise the practice of photomontage in order to make explicit the establishment support for the rise of National Socialism.[9]

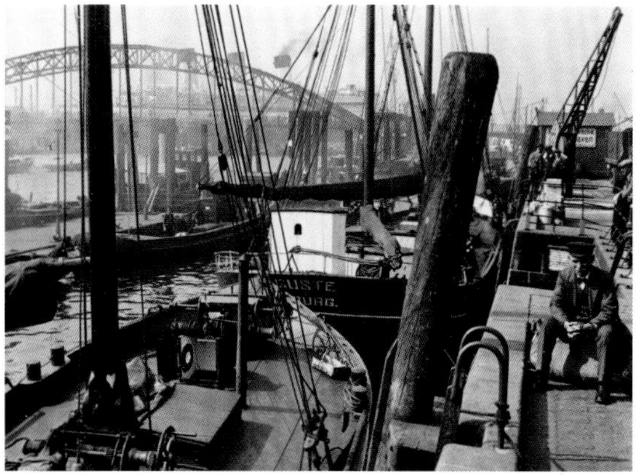

Albert Renger-Patzsch
Hamburg, Port c.1929
Gelatin silver print on paper
16.7 × 23. Tate. Purchased with funds provided by the Photography Acquisitions Committee 2011 [P79960]

If satire in the hands of former dadaists such as Grosz, Dix and Heartfield could expose the political structures that were close to the surface in the Weimar Republic, this frank scrutiny also characterised the less combative realm of portraiture. Both within the practice of painting and, particularly, in photography, the identification of universal 'types' gained ground as a reflection of the very instability of the country's social identity. Photography was well-suited to this balance between portraiture and social investigation, and August Sander's long-running *Menschen des 20. Jahrhunderts* (People of the Twentieth Century) (p.31) came to epitomise a wider practice shared with such diverse contemporaries as Aenne Biermann and Albert Renger-Patzsch.[10] Discussions around 'new photography', to which Roh contributed the famous book *Foto-Auge* ('photo-eye'),[11] ran alongside those about *Neue Sachlichkeit* although they alighted, as Kracauer wrote, on the fact that 'the external likeness achieved by the photograph ... does not readily disclose its internal meaning'.[12]

In portraits connected with magic realism a balance is struck between individuality and anonymity.[13] Some, just as in associated photographs, are seen as 'types' that reflect their purpose as artistic exercises, while those more formally portrayed present themselves self-consciously in anticipation of display. The types are those found in every city: fashionable ladies and shop girls, salesmen and students, prostitutes and drunkards. They are the subject of Grosz's aptly titled '*Der Spiesser-Spiegel*' ('The Mirror of the Bourgeoisie') c.1925 (p.39). They are often anonymous, or effectively so even when named, as they make up the mass of urban population. A fashionable insouciance pervades Jeanne Mammen's women, who balance boredom and the gender ambiguity of the liberated 'new woman' and sexually ambivalent nightlife that so disturbed conservative social commentators (p.79).[14] Those less steely in composure fell by the wayside, like Conrad Felixmüller's beggar collapsed on the cobbled street of Prachatice across the border in the newly formed Czechoslovakia (p.52).

Even as the economic situation eased in the mid-1920s the daily reality for most was concentrated on finding or holding down a job and supporting a family. The singular

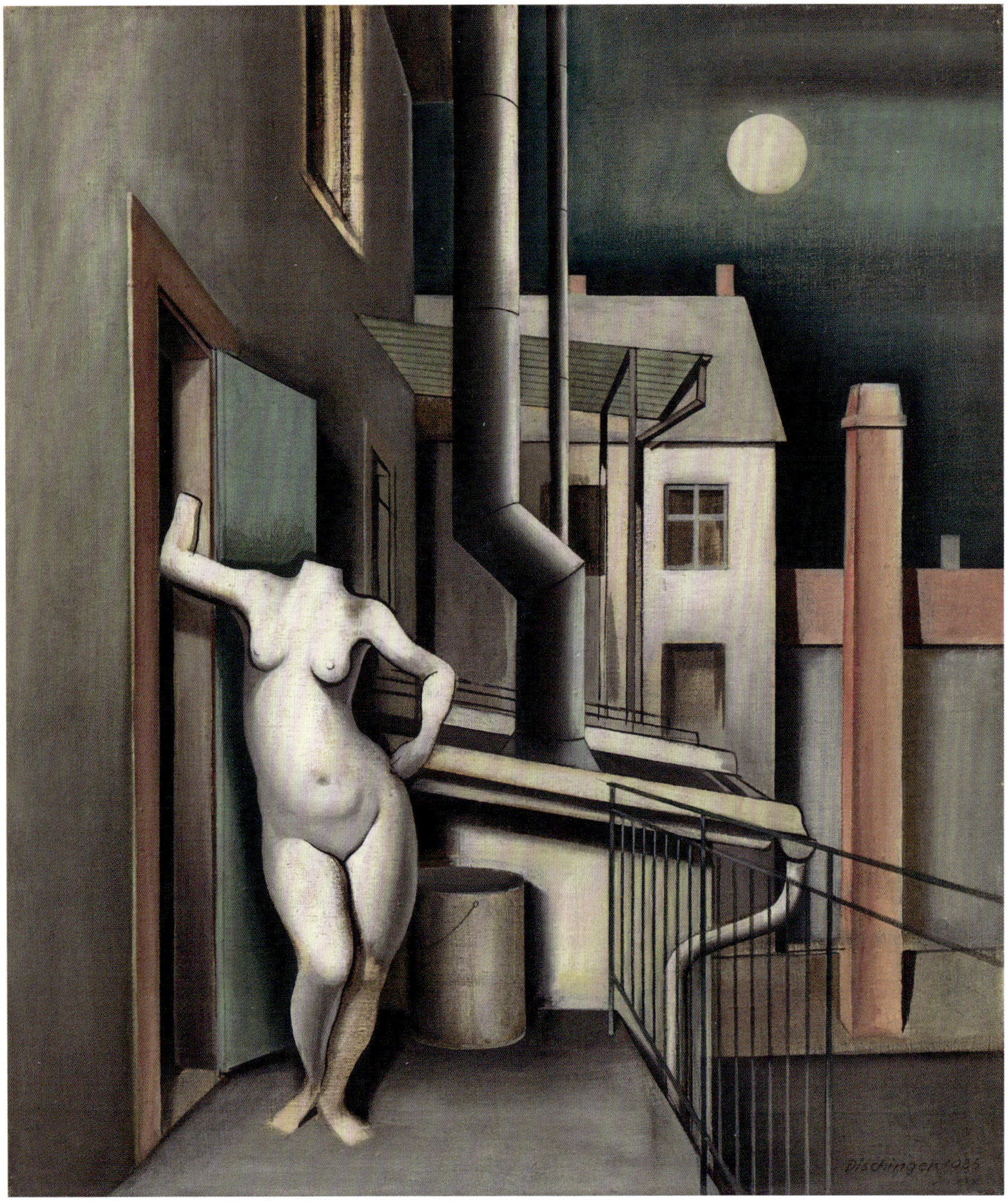

Rudolf Dischinger
Backyard Balcony
Hinterhaus-Balkon 1935
Oil paint on canvas
58 × 50

Opposite page:

Conrad Felixmüller
Portrait of Ernst Buchholz
Bildnis Ernst Buchholz 1921
Oil paint on canvas
90 × 75

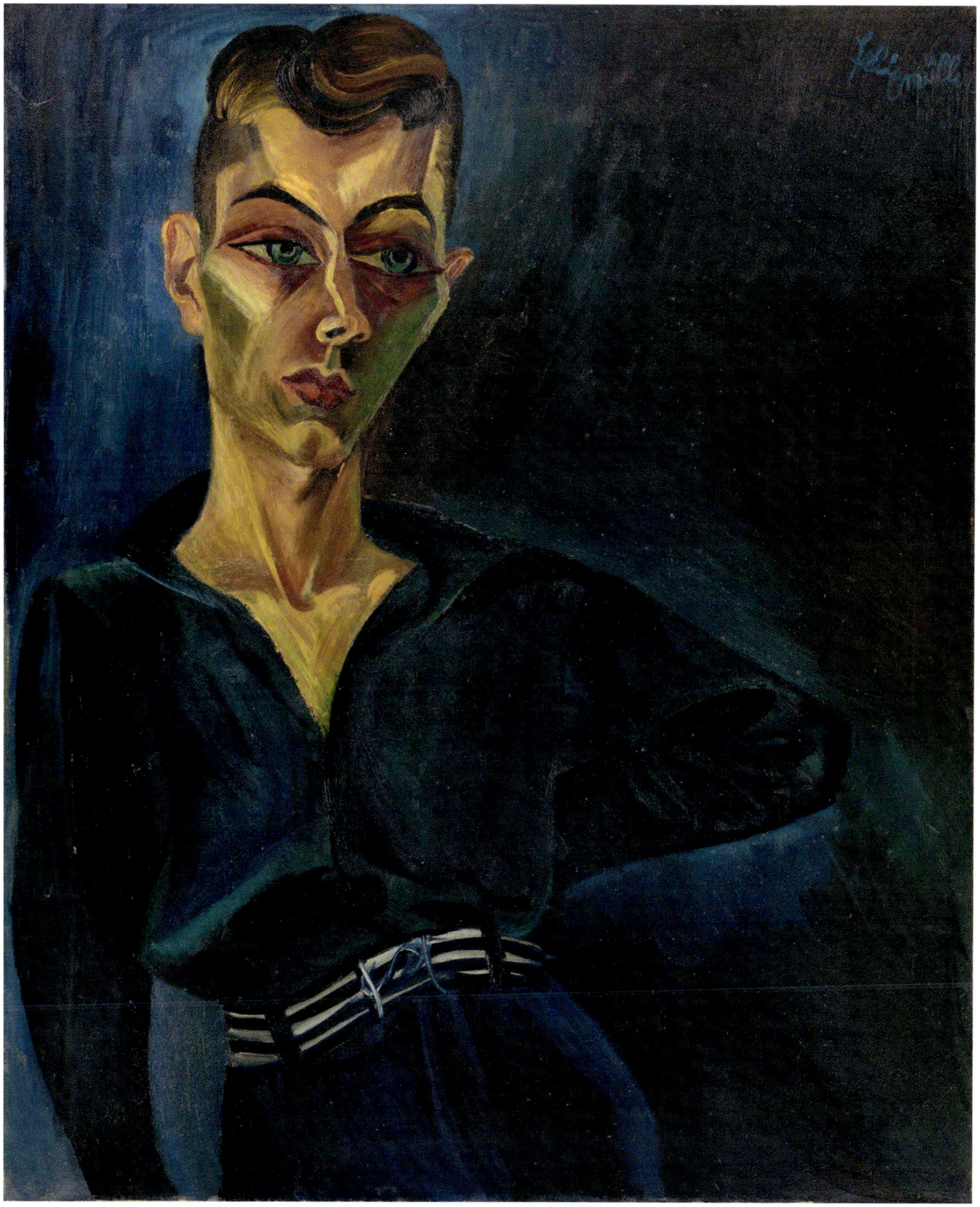

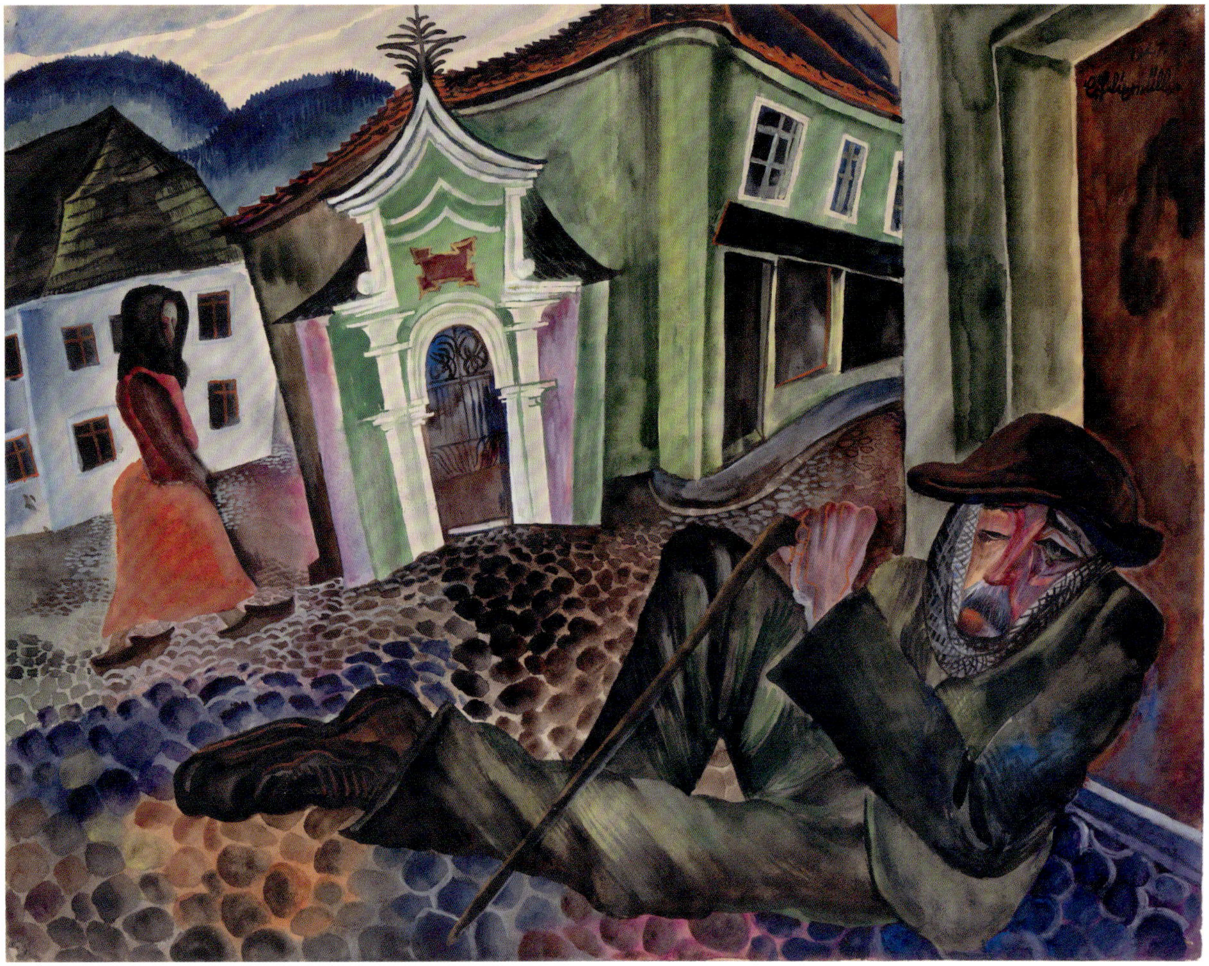

Conrad Felixmüller
The Beggar of Prachatice
Der Bettler von Prachatitz 1924
Watercolour, gouache and graphite on paper
50 × 64.5

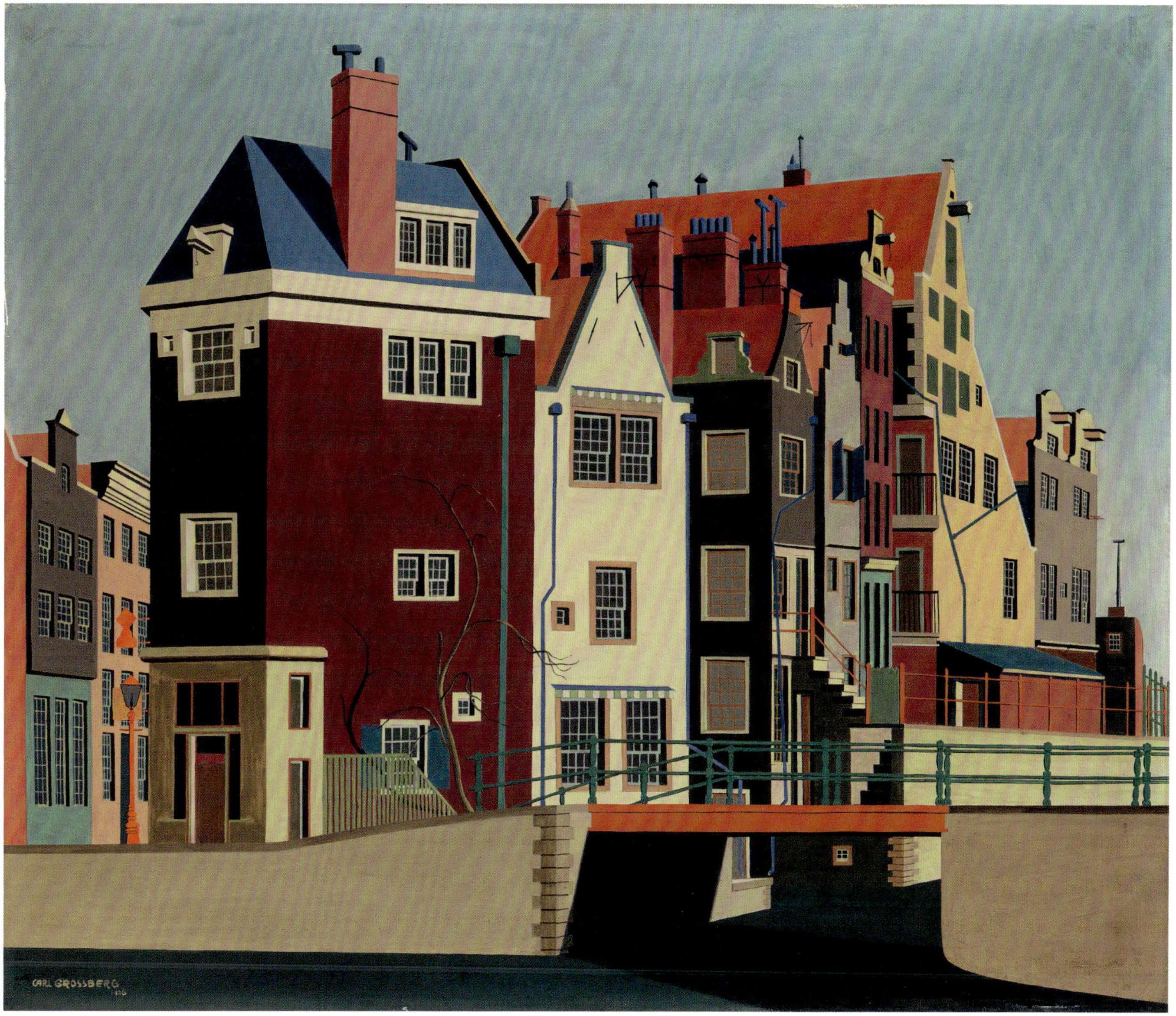

Carl Grossberg
Rokin Street, Amsterdam
Rokin, Amsterdam 1925
Tempera on panel
50.5 × 60.3

sitters are representative of more orthodox types, their character conveyed through their pose, their features and their hands' language of signs. Often in their own self-portraits, the artists identified themselves with these marginal figures, as they don a mask of self-protection or betray the anxieties of existence (pp.13, 41, 60).

Most remarkable are the sitters whose personality transcends the type. The strikingly fur-clad visitor to Paris portrayed by Werner Schramm may be one of those world travellers imagined by Gräff (p.69). The pugnacity of Bruno Alexander Roscher (p.13) is a gift for Dix's satirical precision, just as Schulz suited Birkle's eccentricity (p.23). In *Frauenportrait (Speedy)* (Lady with Red Scarf (Speedy with the Moon)) 1933 (p.67), Rudolf Schlichter renders explicit the confrontational engagement of portraiture. The fact that Speedy was the artist's much-portrayed wife (her Anglicised name displacing Elfriede Koehler) suggests that the fixed stare and self-contained pose go some way to relay their complex creative partnership that Schlichter revealed in his autobiographical books of 1931–2.[15]

Ultimately the passage from the street to the studio was from display to intimacy. The points of reference varied. This is evident in Rudolf Dischinger's *Hinterhaus-Balkon* (Backyard Balcony) 1935 (p.50), where the unprepossessing rear of a tenement is mysteriously inhabited by a headless figure. Whether this is meant to be a classical statue or a dummy, it performs the role of a surrogate human presence that is simultaneously dehumanising. As Richard Müller's *Im Atelier* (In the Studio) 1926 (p.64) demonstrates, the fragmented statues of the classical tradition can prove uncanny even in their more orthodox situation.

Many contemporaries reflected on the intrusion of the sounds and visions of the city, with the window as a repeated means for artists to expose urban compartmentalisation as it eroded the private realm. In his wartime painting, *Selbstmörder* (Suicide) 1916 (p.17), Grosz compounds death and sex in an ambiguous night-time space through which all actions are performed as if on a stage: the man who has blown his brains out and the hanged man appear as if sacrificial victims to the prostitute displaying, and displayed, at the curtained booth. In subsequent works, Grosz habitually showed glimpses into buildings that stacked-up activities of extreme contrast to one another.

Happy Olga! A well-disposed God attached a champagne cork to her soul. Whatever happens, Olga won't go under. She has the most delightful blond hair, the softest, the most radiant blonde's face. She has the most carefree eyes, blue-grey; with cheeky little flecks in the iris. She has the lazy, languorous movements of a harem-girl, and the intellect of a Jewish essayist. She has no ties to anything or anyone, she's the most independent being that Gilgi can imagine ... in the spring Olga will be in Berlin, and then she'll be travelling, here and there, who knows when she'll come back to Cologne. At the moment she's copying a few paintings in the Wallraf-Richartz Museum for an American family. As well as making loud posters for a cinema in Hohestrasse. Olga paints whatever people want. Whether she's a great artist is something which Gilgi can't judge. Olga herself says No. Perhaps she's right. When she needs money, she works; when she has money, she travels. Often unaccompanied, sometimes accompanied.

Irmgard Keun, *Gilgi, eine von uns*, Berlin 1931, translated as *Gilgi, One of Us* by Geoff Wilkes, Brooklyn and London 2013, p.18

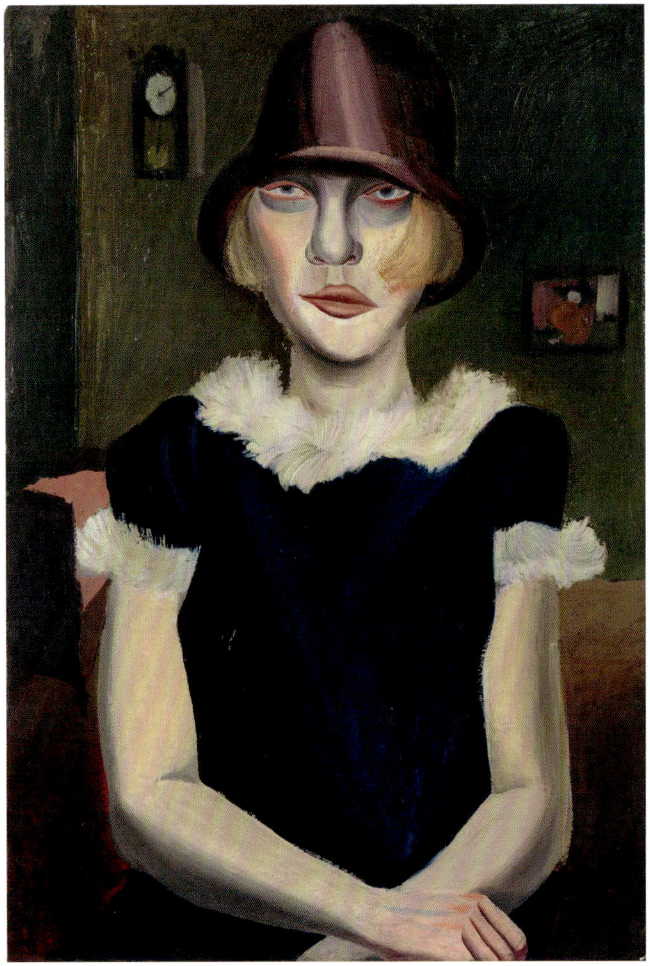

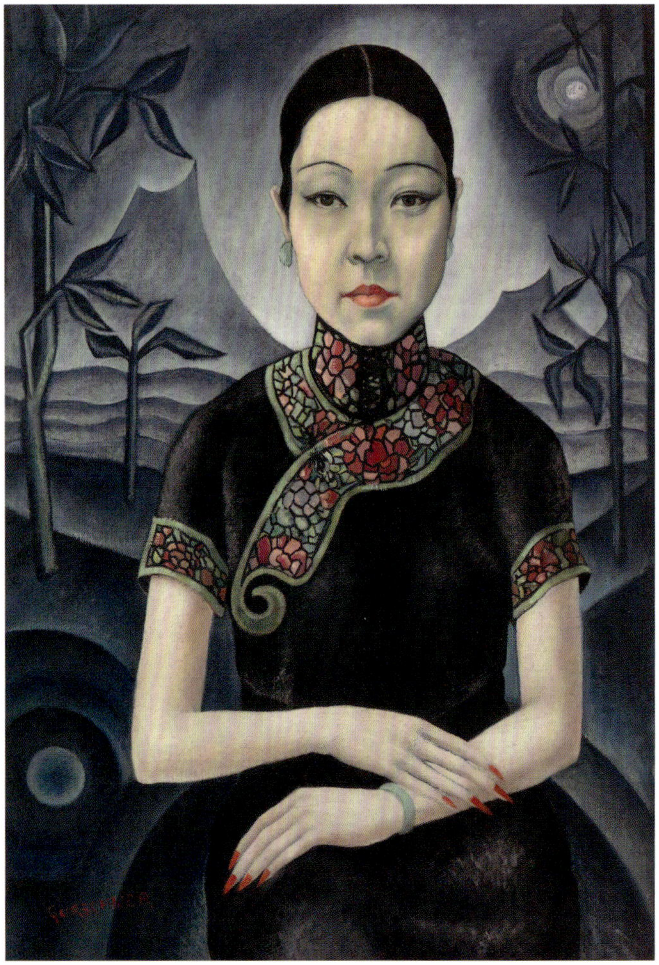

Hans Grundig
Girl with Pink Hat
Mädchen mit rosa Hut 1925
Oil paint on cardboard
70.4 × 50

Herbert Gurschner
Japanese Lady
Japanische Dame 1932
Oil paint on canvas
87 × 61

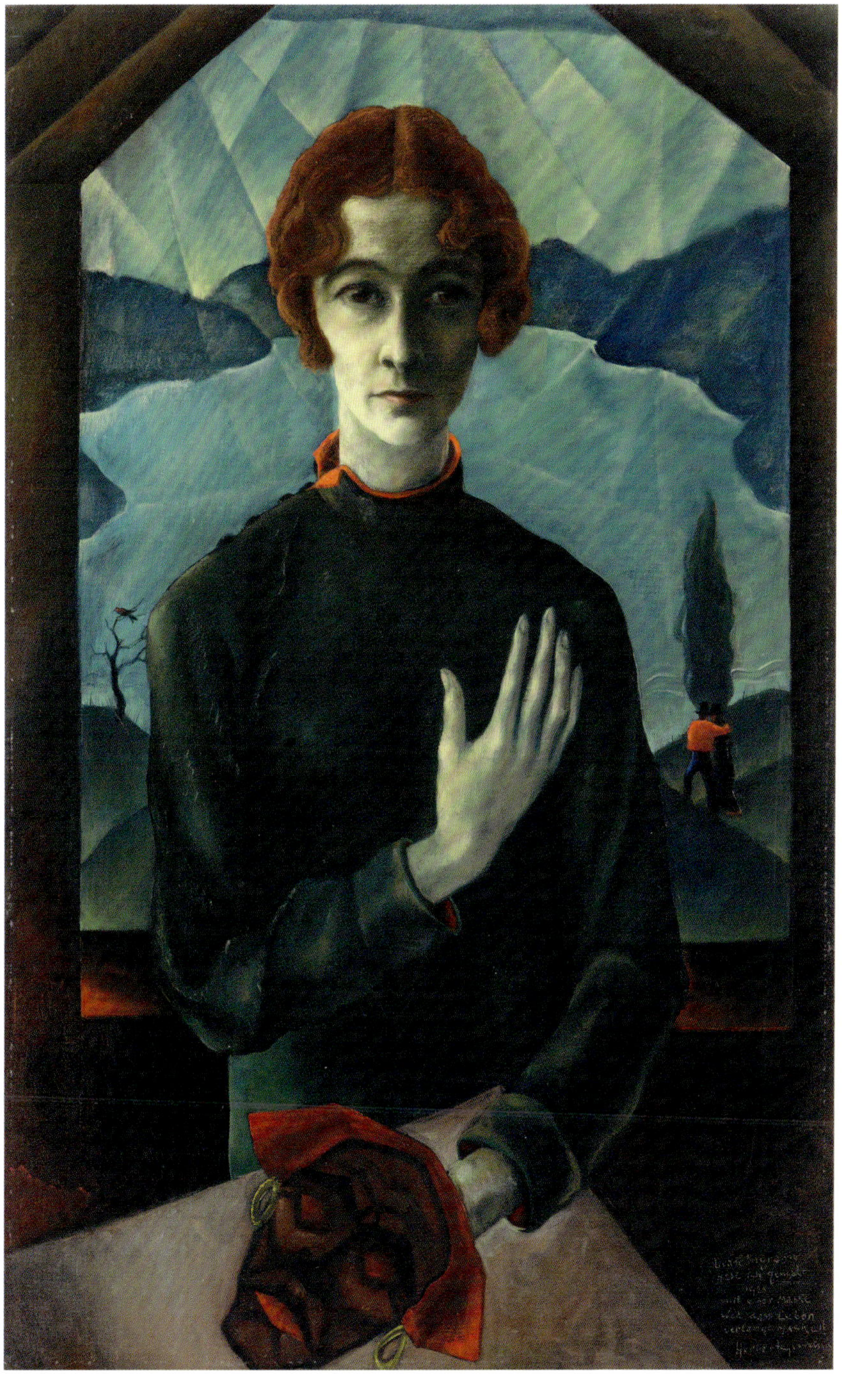

Herbert Gurschner
Bean Ingram 1928
Oil paint on canvas
107 × 67.5

Within the studio, the artist could retreat into concentration: a zone of intimacy in which the classical concern with the nude converted into something starker. This is evident in the contrast between Müller's studio peopled by classical statues and the challenging nudity of Otto Rudolf Schatz's *Mondfrauen* (Moon Women) 1930 (p.66). Presented with few classical allusions (beyond the drapery behind them), these women are like pneumatic fantasy figures. Two disarmingly real nudes appear, in contrast, in Otto Griebel's *Zwei Frauen* (Two Women) 1924 (p.77). The women's defiant frontality was a device (albeit for clothed men) to which Griebel returned in his most famous painting, *Die Internationale* (The Internationale) 1929. Both depict solidarity among workers that anticipates the socialist realism of the 1930s, but, while not depicting the visceral violence of the *lustmord* works common to the period, *Two Women* is clearly imbued with a sense of misogyny and exploitation.[16] More orthodox in its depiction of studio-bound nudes is Franz Radziwill's *Gespräch über einen Paragraphen* (Conversation about a Paragraph) 1929 (p.65). Although it was begun just after Radziwill had completed his period of study with Dix in Dresden, it shows his own characteristically sharp colours and habit of contrasting the lit foreground with distant darkness. This was seen most often in detailed, if disconcertingly threatening, landscapes. Although the tiny angel that floats above the reclining nude was added when Radziwill returned to the painting in later life, the detail serves to heighten the uncanny atmosphere already present in the original.

Reflecting in 1933 on the broad trajectory of Hartlaub's *Neue Sachlichkeit*, the British critic Herbert Read remarked that 'such realism, sardonic in its essence, is not likely to be acceptable to those who want art to be pretty, or even to be beautiful in the classic sense'. Noting Beckmann and Dix, he offered Grosz as symptomatic of the much wider attitude, and concluded that the painter, 'by attacking the most deeply seated hypocrisies of our social life, our habitual sensualities, can only be accepted in a mood of spiritual asceticism, though everywhere his sensitive technique has its fine surgical beauty'.[17] In so doing, Read identified the apparently paradoxical gulf that had been opened between precision and beauty in relation to the new realism.

MG

Local News

It was the second week in April, when the weather in Berlin is sometimes spring-like, and, as the press unanimously stated, this splendid Easter weather lured people out-of-doors. In Berlin, at that time, Alex Fränkel, a Russian student, shot and killed Vera Kaminskaya, his fiancée, aged twenty-two, arts-and-crafts worker, in their boarding-house. Tatiana Sanftleben, same age, a governess, who had agreed to join in the suicide pact, became afraid of this decision at the last moment and ran away when she saw her girl-friend lying on the floor. She met a squad of police to whom she told the story of her terrible experience of the last few months, and led the officers to the place where Vera and Alex were lying mortally wounded. The criminal police were called in and the murder squad dispatched its officers to the spot. Alex and Vera had planned to get married, but economic conditions did not permit their conjugal union.

... the investigation into the question of responsibility for the tram-car disaster in Heerstrasse is not yet completed. The examination of the victims and of Redlich, the conductor, is still proceeding. The opinions of the technical experts have not yet been received. Only after their receipt will it be possible to enter upon an examination of the question whether any blame attaches to the conductor, because he applied the brakes too late, or whether it was a concatenation of unfortunate circumstances that caused the disaster.

Quiet conditions prevailed in the stock market; open stock prices were steadier in view of the Reichsbank statement about to be published, which is said to show a very favourable state of affairs with a reduction in the banknote circulation of 400 millions and a reduction in the exchange situation of 350 millions. Quotations on April 18 about 11 o'clock were: I.G. Dye Stuffs 260½ to 267, Siemens & Halske 297½ to 299, Dessauer Gas 202 to 203, Waldhof Cellulose 295. Bids for German Oil at 134½.

... On April 11, Herr Braun, editor, was liberated from Moabit Prison by an armed party. It was a regular Wild West scene. A search is being made for them. The Acting President of the Criminal Court immediately made a report on the matter to the superior authorities. Meanwhile the examination of eye-witnesses and the officials involved continues.

Alfred Döblin, *Berlin, Alexanderplatz: Die Geschichte vom Franz Biberkopf*, Berlin 1929, translated as *Berlin, Alexanderplatz: The Story of Franz Biberkopf* by Eugene Jolas, London 1931, Harmondsworth 1978, pp.197–8.

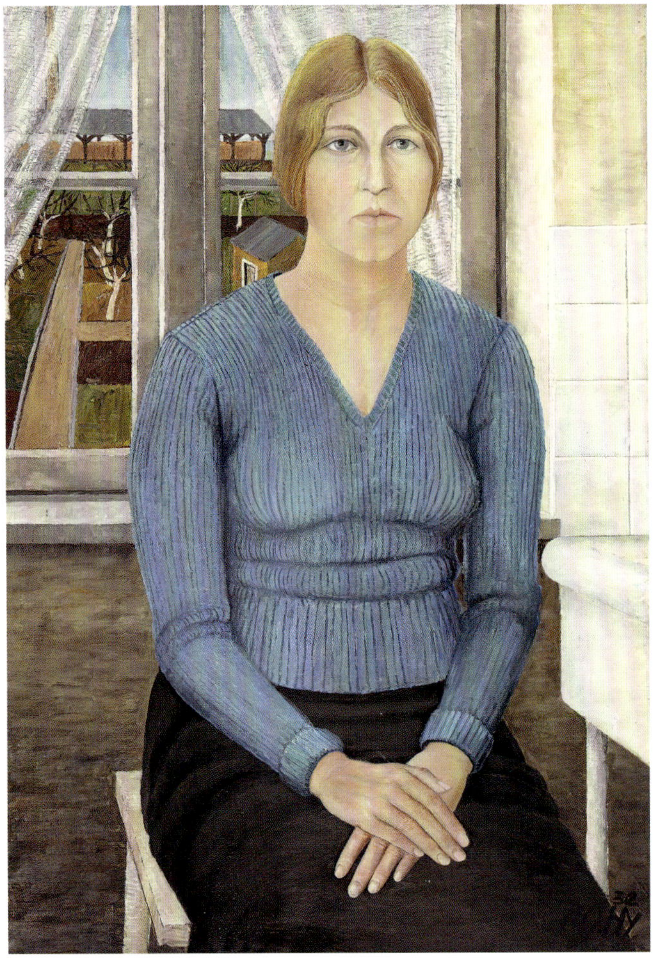

Karl Otto Hy
Anna 1932
Oil paint on canvas
95 × 67.5

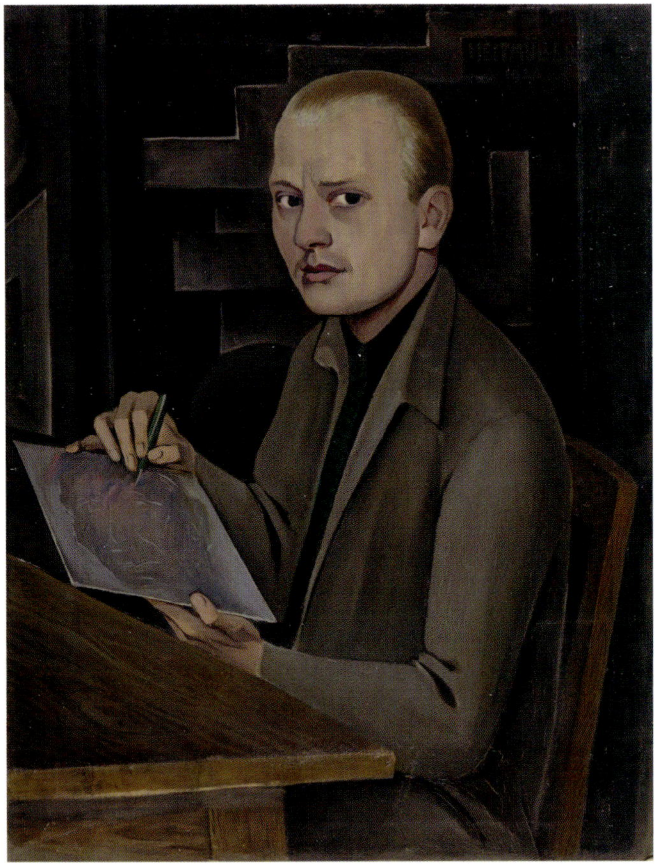

August Heitmüller
Self-Portrait
Selbstbildnis 1926
Oil paint on canvas
90 × 70.5

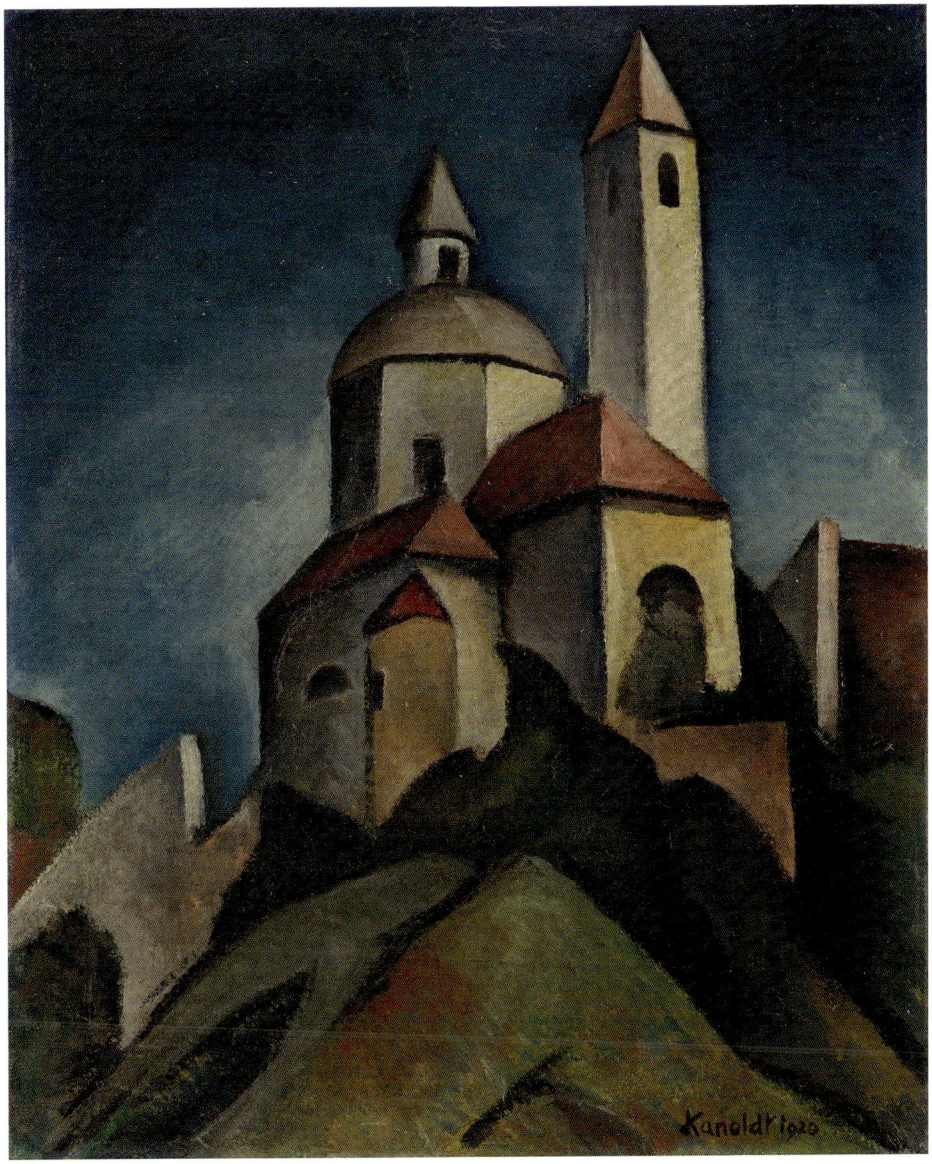

Alexander Kanoldt
Monastery Chapel of Säben
Kapelle in Südtirol 1920
Oil paint on canvas
35 × 29

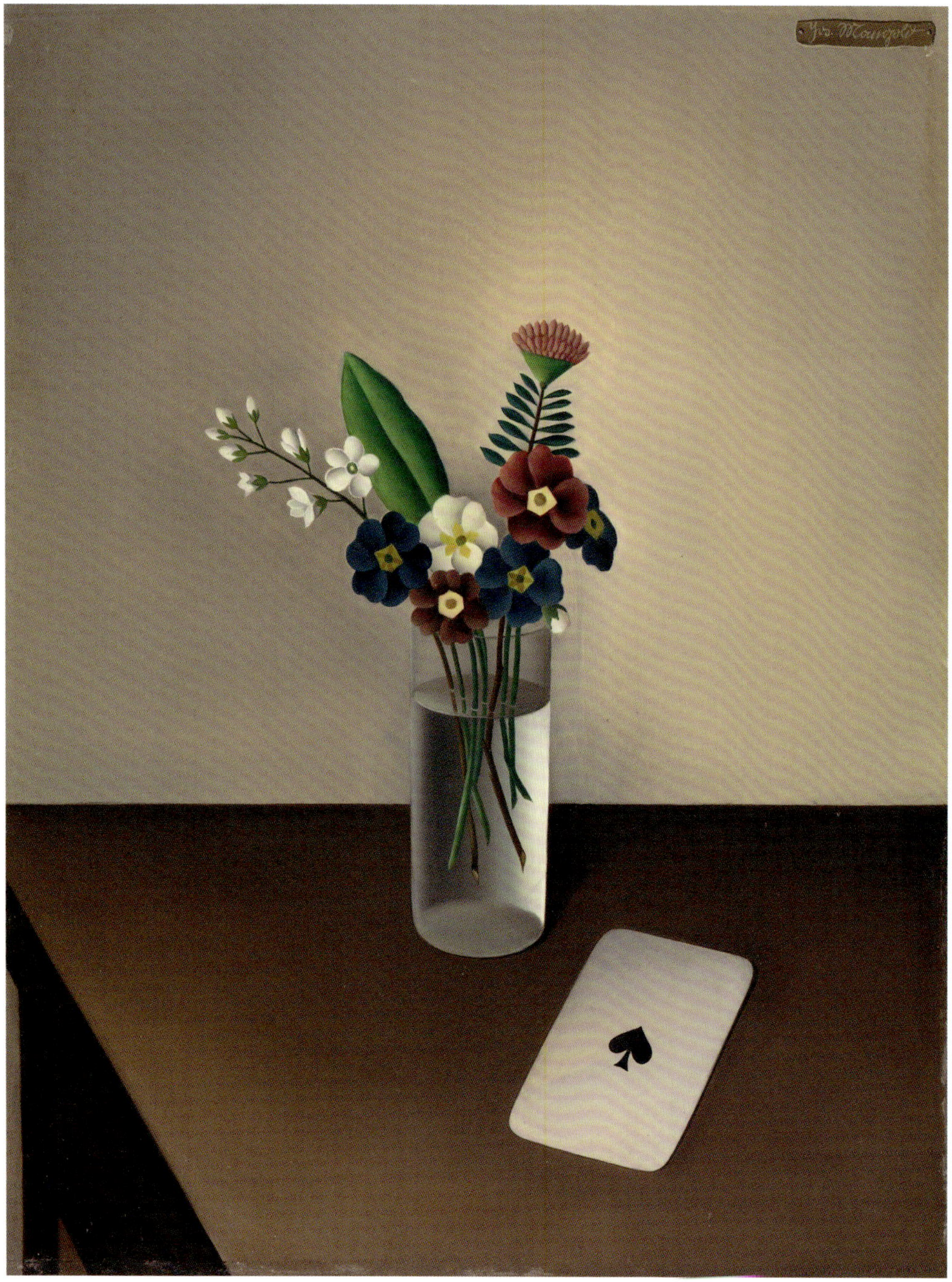

Josef Mangold
Flower Still Life with Playing Card
Blumenstilleben mit Spielkarte
undated
Oil paint on panel
41 × 51.7

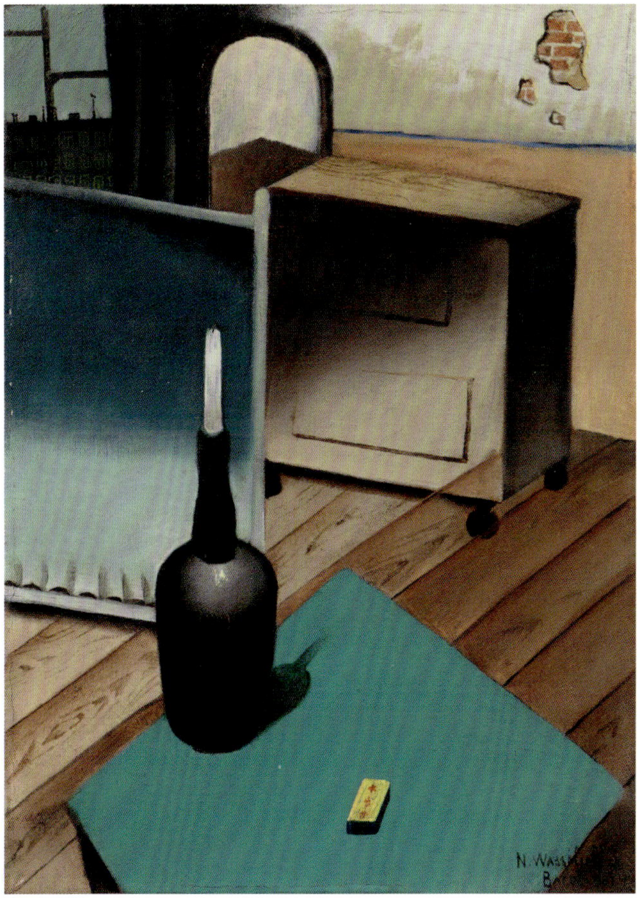

Nicolai Wassilieff
Interior
Innere 1923
Oil paint on canvas
41 × 30

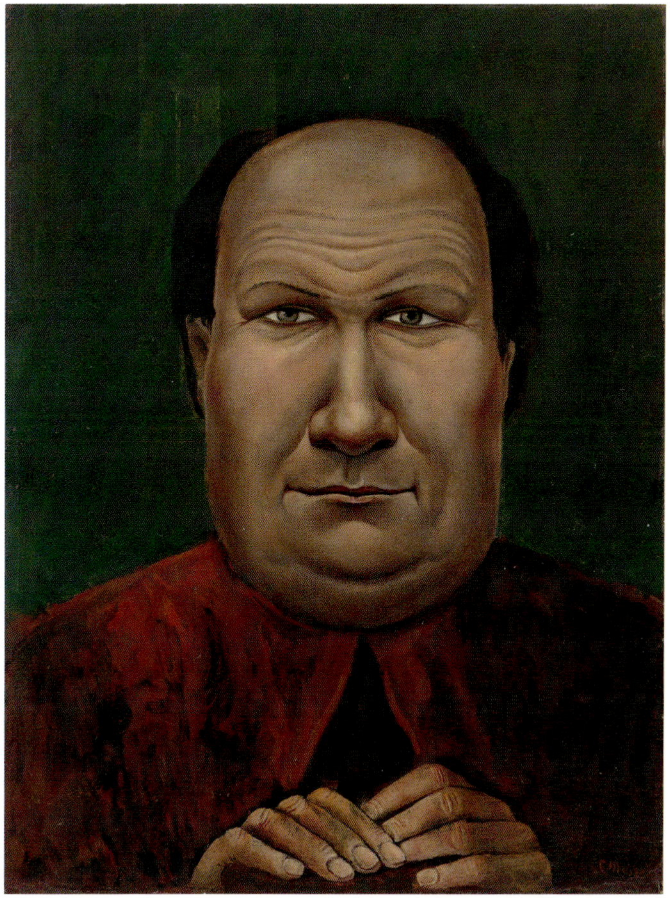

Carlo Mense
Portrait of Don Domenico
Bildnis Don Domenico 1924
Oil paint on cardboard
53.6 × 42

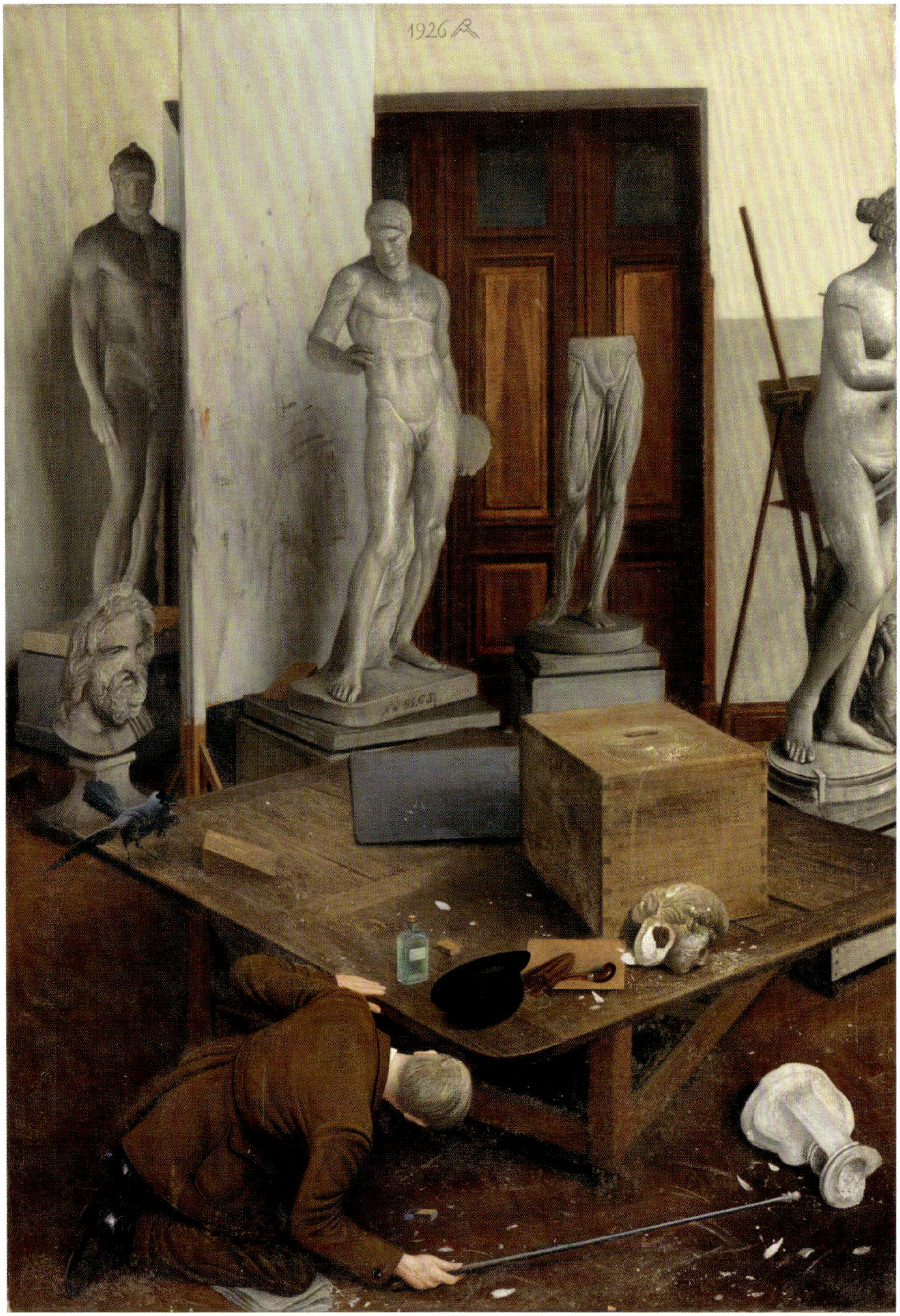

Richard Müller
In the Studio
Im Atelier 1926
Oil paint on canvas
107 × 75.5

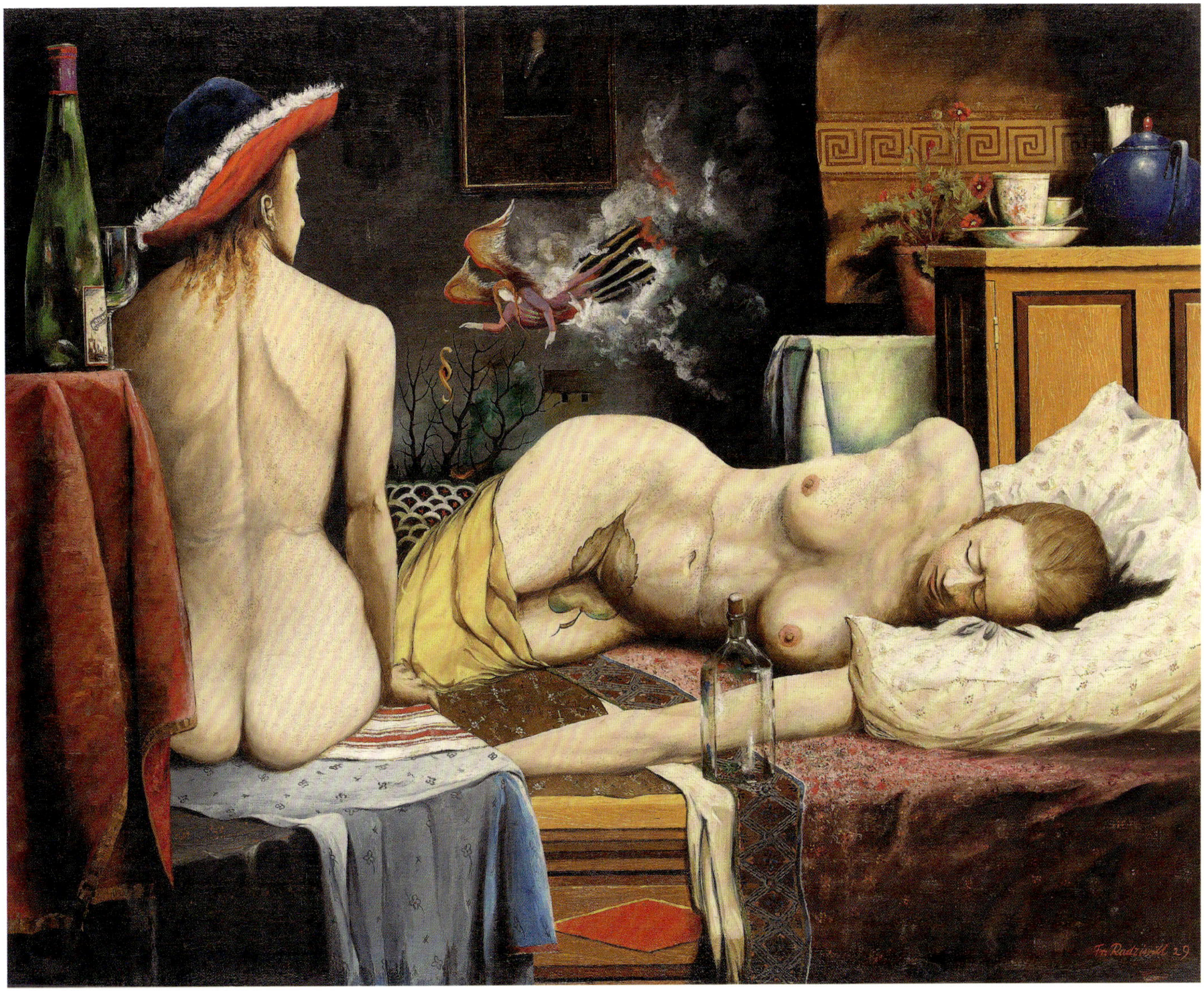

Franz Radziwill
Conversation about a Paragraph
Gespräch über einen Paragraphen 1929
Oil paint on canvas laid on wood
79.3 × 101

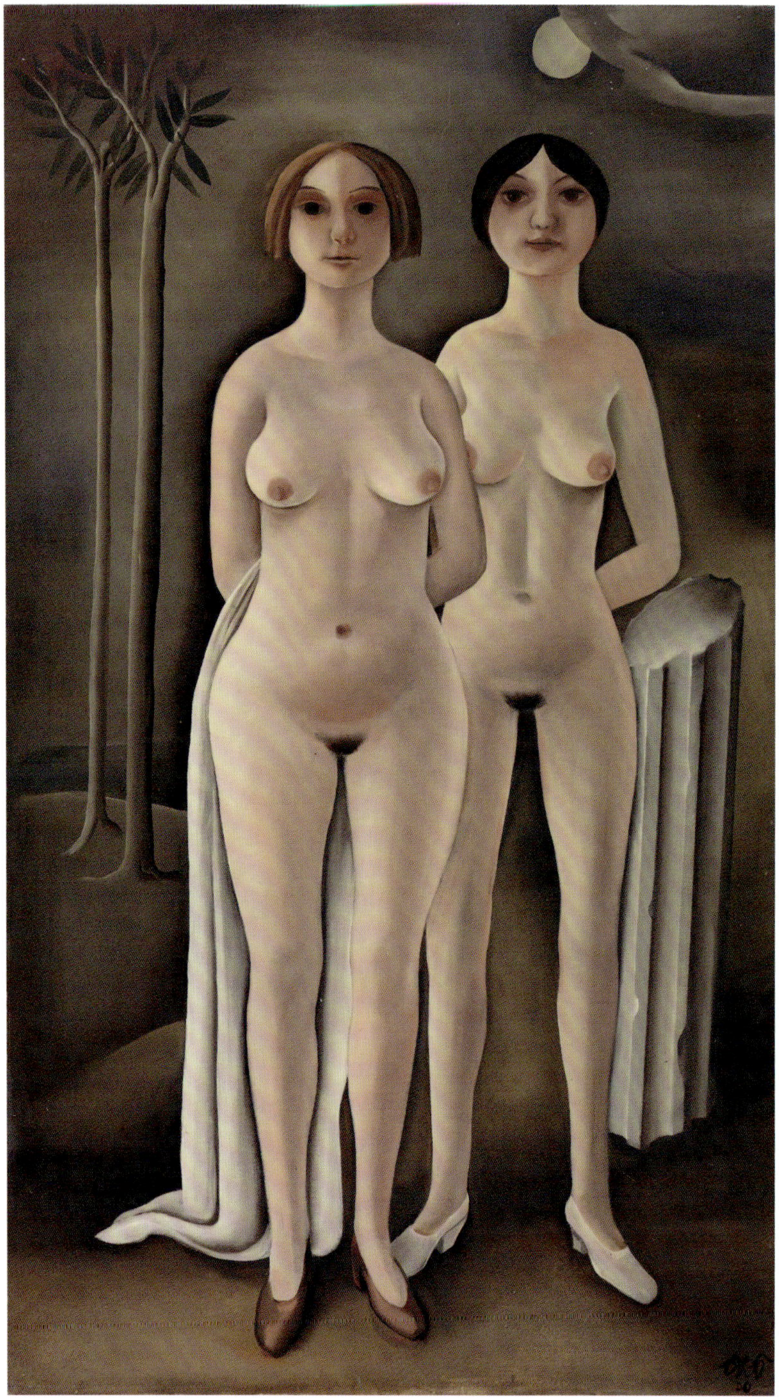

Otto Rudolf Schatz
Moon Women
Mondfrauen 1930
Oil paint on canvas
191.5 × 111

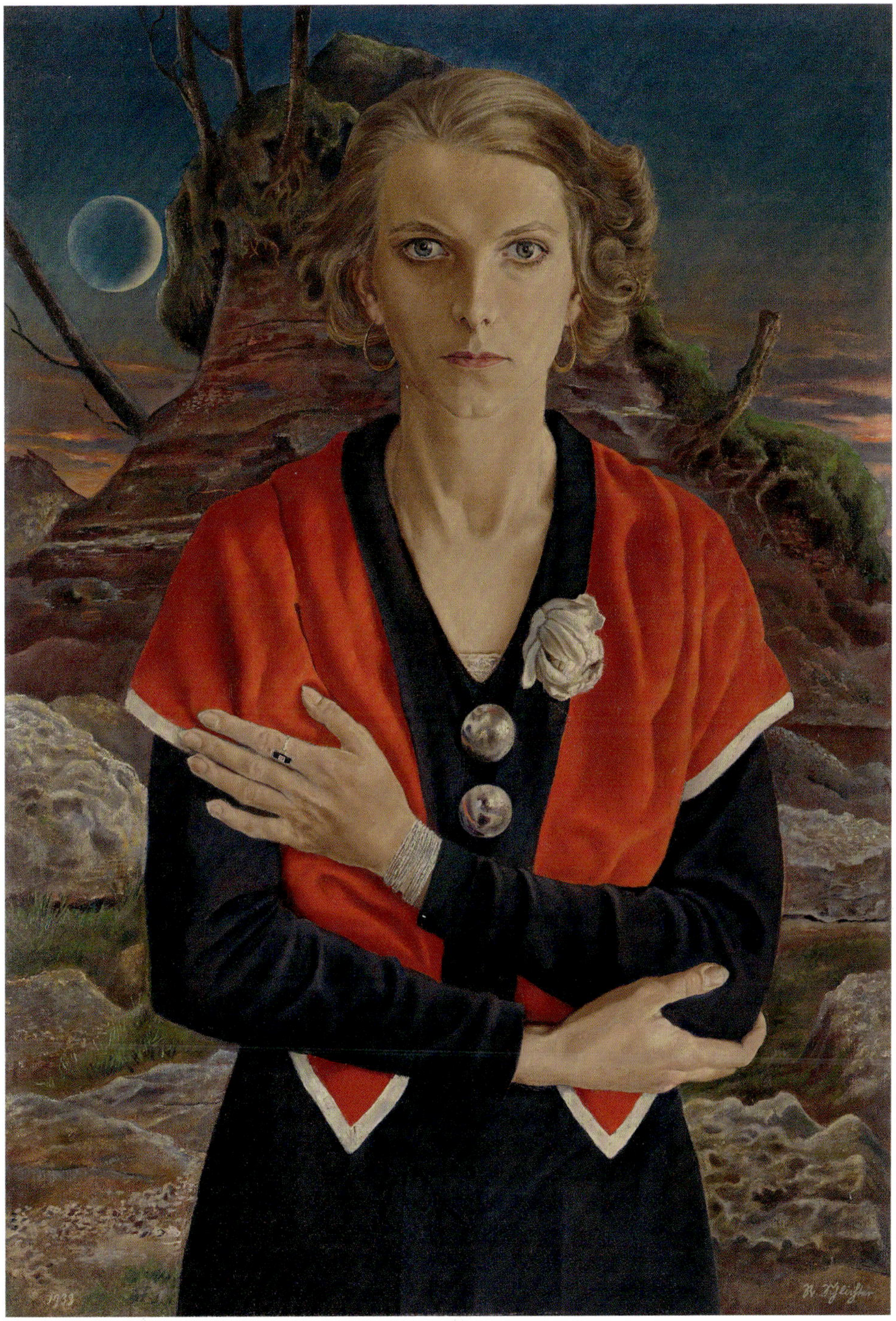

Rudolf Schlichter
Lady with Red Scarf
(Speedy with the Moon)
Frauenportrait (Speedy) 1933
Oil paint on canvas
92.5 × 64.5

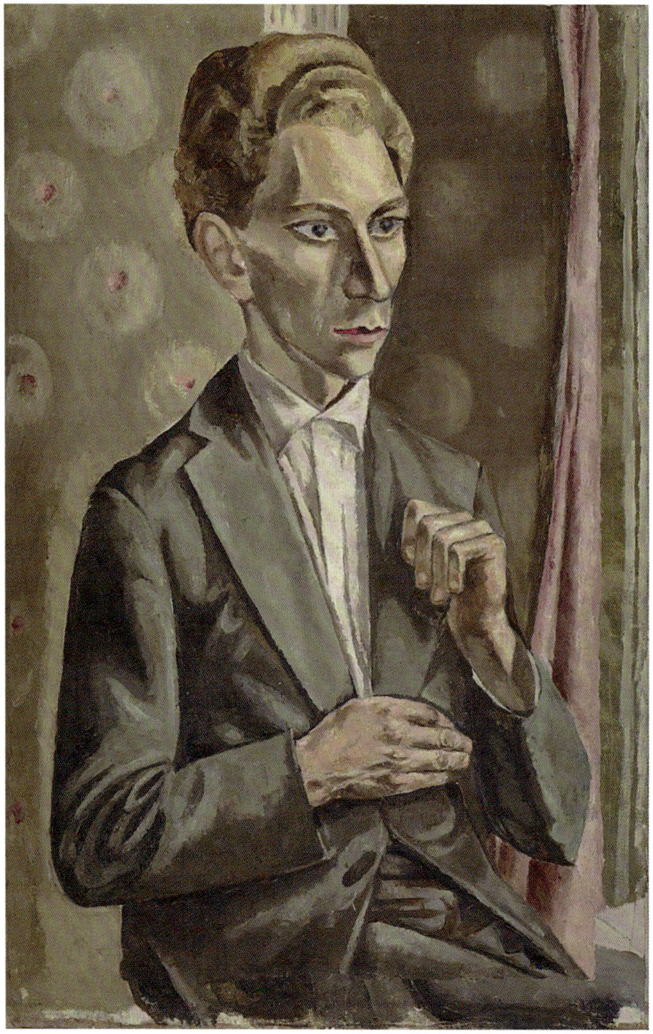

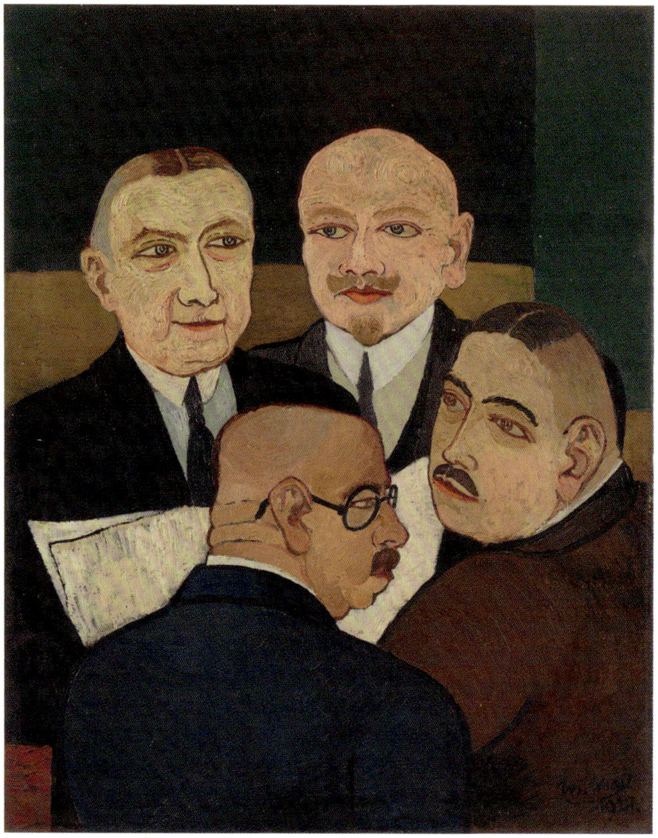

Marie-Louise von Motesiczky
Portrait of a Russian Student
Porträt eines russischen Studenten 1927
Oil paint on canvas
82.8 × 54.2

Josef Scharl
Conference / The Group
Konferenz / Die Gruppe 1927
Oil paint on canvas
81 × 64.5

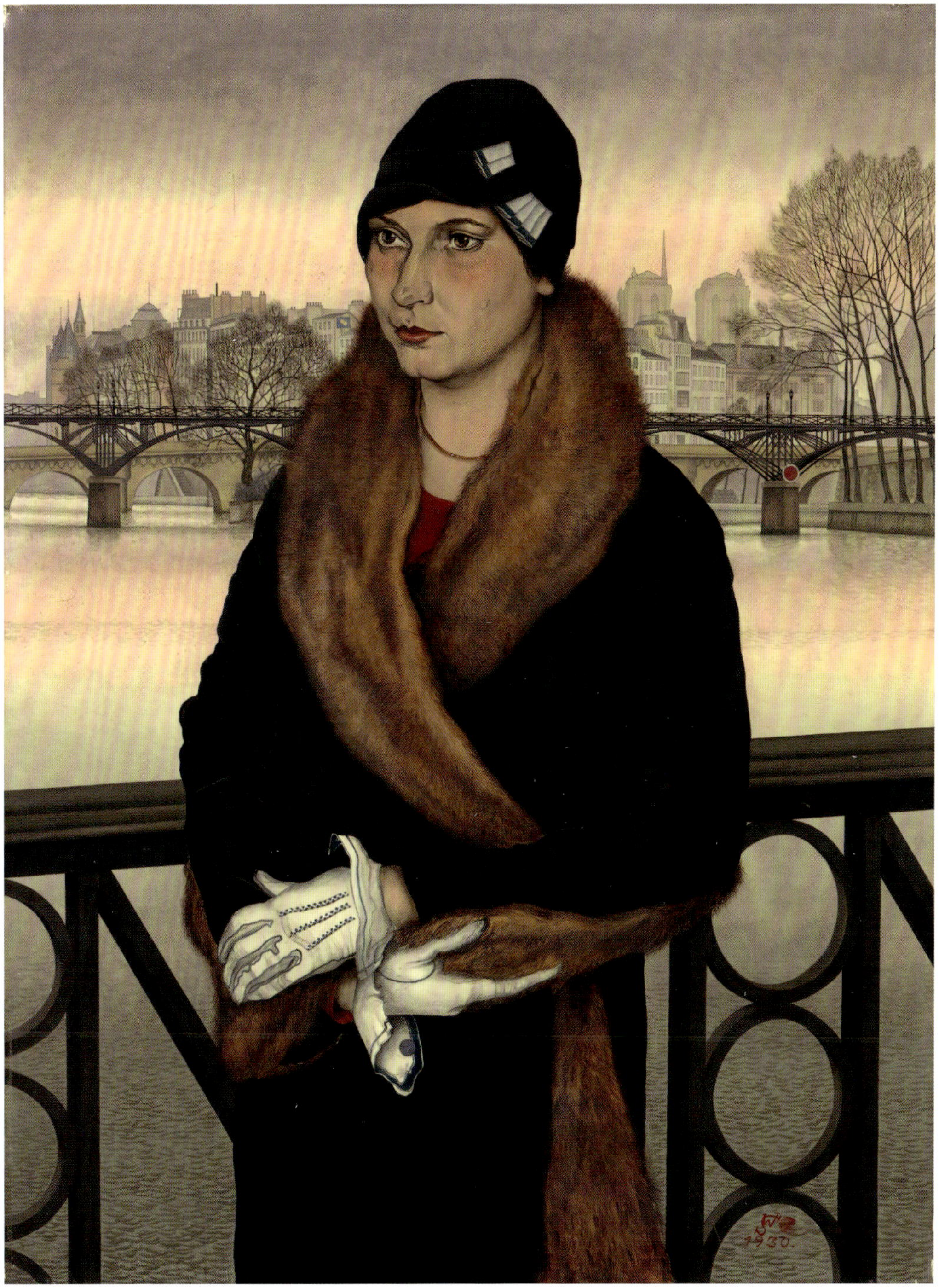

Werner Schramm
Portrait of a Lady in front of the Pont des Arts
Damenbildnis vor der Pont des Arts 1930
Oil paint on panel
81 × 61

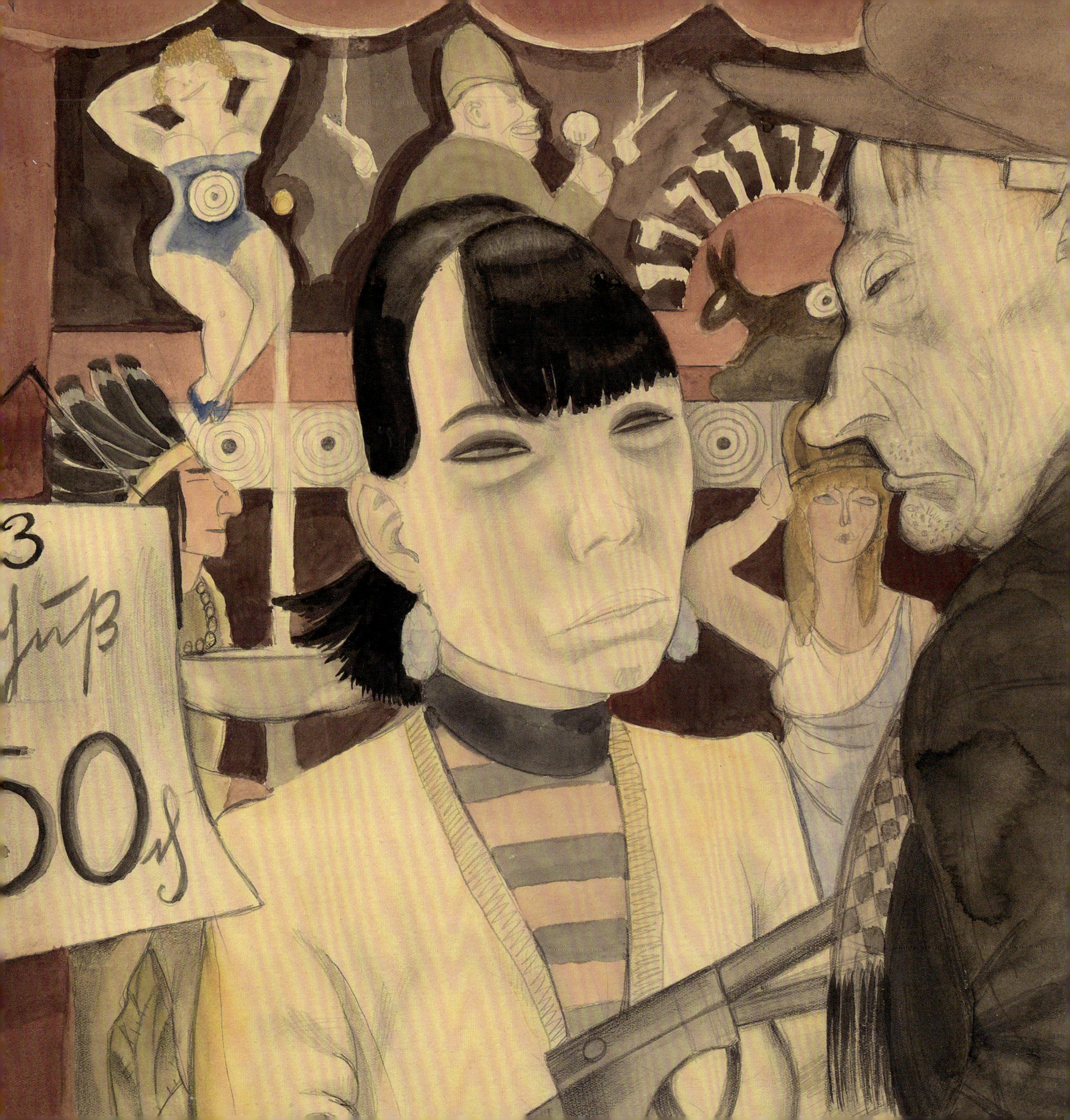

3
50

The Cabaret: 'Looking for Adventure'

> Every city has an official and an unofficial side, and it is superfluous to add that the latter is more interesting and more informative of the essence of a city. That which appears so clearly in the light of the arc lamps has a face more like a mask than a physiognomy. The smile it offers is more an appeal to the visitor's purse. It wears the makeup of the coquette, applied too thickly to permit the true features underneath to be recognised. Those who are looking for adventure, who hope for sensations – they must go into the shadows.[1]

In this way, the writer Curt Moreck describes the hidden side of a city that thrives beneath the veneer of polite society. That the anthropomorphised city is Berlin, a decade into the Weimar period, is crucial – especially given that Moreck's text was essentially a guide to homosexual venues in defiance of the fact that homosexuality remained formally outlawed in Germany. Moreck's book runs parallel to contemporary artistic depictions of the clubs and cabarets that were indicative of a strong cross-cultural and non-binary dialogue, transcending the borders of the Republic but also inhibited by the limitations of the entrenched gender roles of the time.

The cabaret has its roots in seventeenth-century Paris, but first emerged in Germany in 1901 with the founding of the Überbrettl in Berlin by Ernst von Wolzogen.[2] Those of Weimar Germany had their own unique identity: sometimes distinguished as *Kabarett* (with a 'k'), and comprising content that was predominantly satirical in nature, parodying social and political situations. With foundations as a pan-European, counter-cultural phenomenon, these cabarets were built on outward-looking and tolerant values. They reflected the way in which German artists' engagement with international culture extended beyond performance. After all, it was during this same moment that artists described in Franz Roh's text on the new phenomenon of 'magic realism' were drawing upon external inspirations: these ranged from the influence of Giorgio de Chirico's *Arte metafisica* in the evocation of uncanny spaces to the acute attention to physiognomy found in Northern European painting of the Renaissance.

Any exposition on the visual history of cabaret and nightclubs, whether French or German, poses some intriguing challenges. Due to the centrality of live performance there are few archival remnants, and as such the cabaret might be described as a transient art

Detail, see p.79

form: an identification that resists leaving a trace in posterity. The sites were intimate settings for social gatherings, with a separate and distinct identity from the formal music revues designed to appeal to larger audiences. The underground and often politically subversive nature of the entertainments meant that the spaces of the cabaret could be clearly identified as spaces of permissiveness. Even if desirable, the dimly lit, action-based performances and settings of the cabaret were difficult to photograph. It is notable that the photographs of Zurich and Berlin dada performances, or Oskar Schlemmer's *Baukastenspiel* (Block Play) performed at the Bauhaus in 1926,[3] are clearly enacted for the camera.

The popularity of the cabaret is partly attributable to a new air of tolerance in the postwar moment, and the desire for individuals to enjoy life's fleeting pleasures. During the unprecedented hyperinflation of 1922–3, when one US dollar was equivalent to four billion German marks, clients of the cabaret were determined to reap the hedonistic benefits of their cash before it became devalued the following day. Robert McAlmon, the American writer drawn to Berlin by the strength of the dollar, characterised this unstable world:

> At nights along the Unter den Linden it was never possible to know whether it was a woman or a man in woman's clothes who accosted one. That didn't matter, but it was sad to know that innumerable young and normal Germans were doing anything, from dope selling to every form of prostitution, to have money for themselves and for their families, their widowed mothers and younger brothers and sisters.[4]

Such profligacy and folly became the subjects of performances.[5] As a consequence, knowledge is mediated primarily through written accounts or through reimaginings on film, and crucially, each with an international link. In the public imagination, knowledge of the cabaret was mainly cinematic, with the spectral form of Marlene Dietrich in the 1930 *Der Blaue Engel* (The Blue Angel) having particular resonance. From Christopher Isherwood's autobiographical novel *Goodbye to Berlin* 1939, there proliferated a lineage of adaptations: the first was in the theatre in John Van Druten's 1951 play *I Am a Camera*, and then in Bob Fosse's 1972 film *Cabaret*, in which Liza Minnelli dazzled as the brazen Sally Bowles: a further reinvention, in evoking the Weimar movie star Louise Brooks. The effect

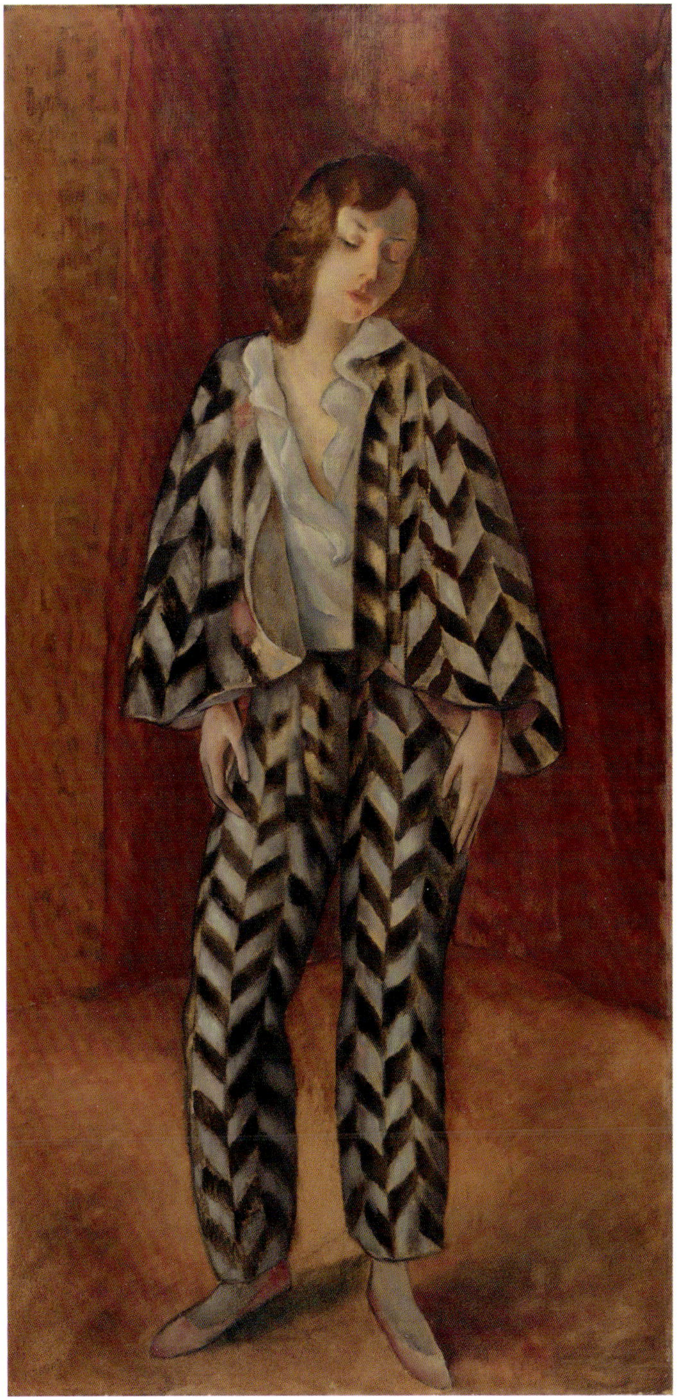

Josef Eberz
Dancer (Beatrice Mariagraete)
Tänzerin (Beatrice Mariagraete)
1923
Oil paint on canvas
158 × 78.5

of this repeated filtering and mediation encouraged the notion that cabaret itself was somewhat heretic, its notoriety being mythologised by those privileged enough to have been witnesses.

Artistic depictions of urban entertainment capture both performers and spectators, forming part of a trans-European legacy dating back through the work of Ernst Ludwig Kirchner in Dresden and Berlin, and Kees van Dongen in Paris, and even further back into the nineteenth century through the work of Georges Seurat and Edgar Degas.[6] These artists exposed the illusion of performance by looking beyond the stage, capturing the expressions and salacious behaviour of the sometimes conspicuously inattentive audience.

Continuing in this tradition, cross-cultural pollinations are evident in a number of paintings from the Weimar period. The subject of Josef Eberz's portrait *Tänzerin (Beatrice Mariagraete)* (Dancer (Beatrice Mariagraete)) 1923 (p.73), was originally from Sweden but came to be associated with the pioneering *Münchener Tranzgruppe* (which had originated in Hamburg), among other choreographic societies in Germany.[7] Referencing the male Harlequin of the commedia dell'arte, Mariagraete's chevron-patterned attire carries tentative allusions to androgyny.[8]

Likewise, Prosper de Troyer's portrait *Erik Satie (Le prélude)* (Eric Satie (The Prelude)) 1925 is indicative of a dialogue that transcends national borders, in the biographies of both the artist and subject, and the content of the painting (p.75). The Belgian de Troyer admired the writings and theories of Filippo Tommaso Marinetti, the Italian poet and founder of futurism, and experimented with a dynamic abstraction. In de Troyer's monumental painting of Satie, the avant-garde composer is shown conducting a pianist. The scene is complicated by the reflection of the audience in the polished lid of the piano, some of whom appear lost in the musical reverie with eyes closed or head in hands. Behind the grand piano are two women of different ethnicities – one with dark skin, who turns the music, and the other fair, holding a halo above the composer's head – a likely reference to Satie's death on 1 July 1925.

Although painted much later in Amsterdam, Max Beckmann's *Anni (Mädchen mit Fächer)* (Anni (Girl with Fan)) 1942 (p.77) is a nostalgic recollection of a typical scene in a Monte Carlo nightclub, in which a young woman's face is softly illuminated during

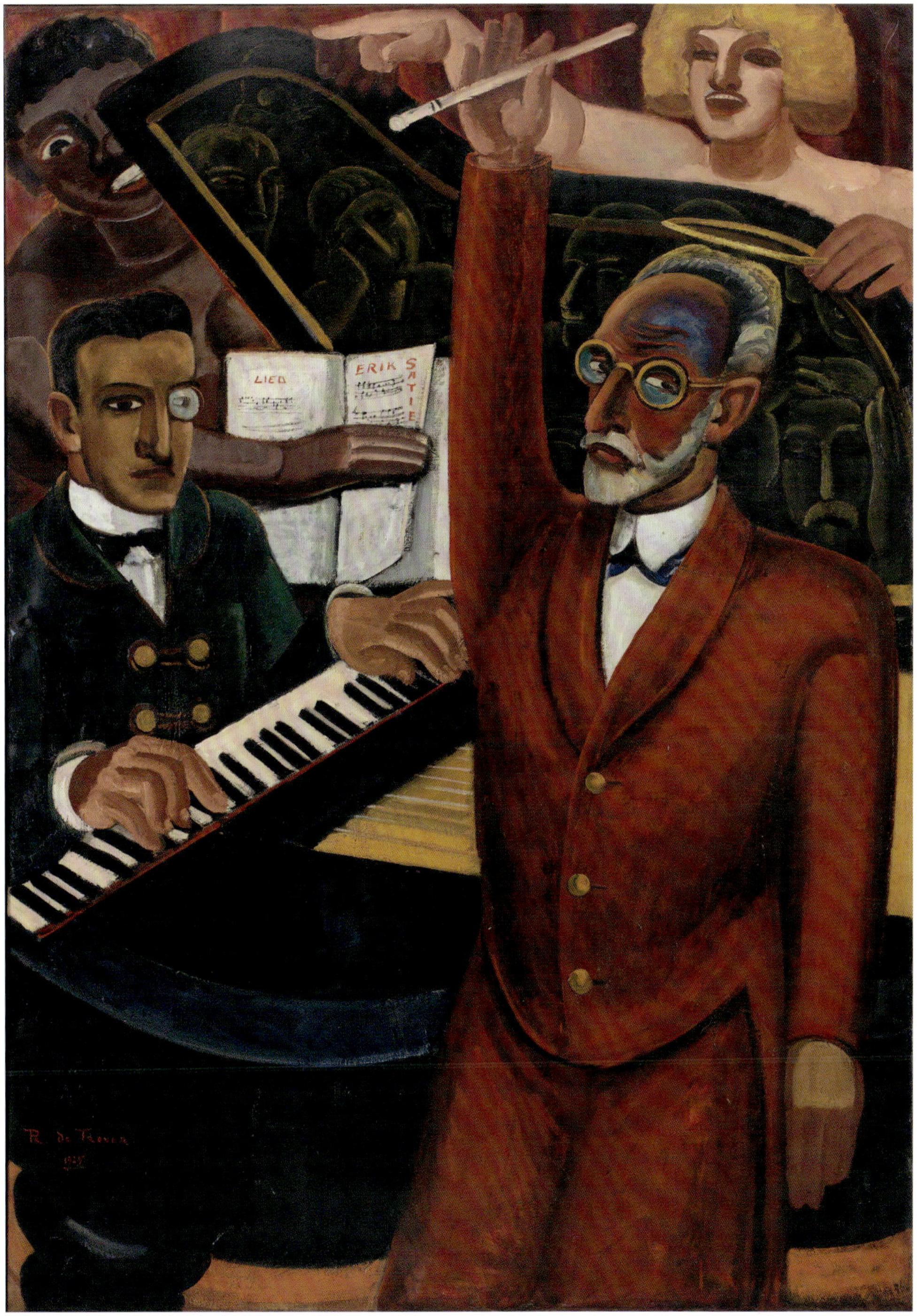

Prosper de Troyer
Erik Satie (The Prelude)
Erik Satie (Le prélude) 1925
Oil paint on canvas
210 × 145

a nocturnal liaison. Beckmann touches upon intimacy and seduction, showing Anni apparently engaged with a male companion but nonetheless gazing out at the viewer, who is rendered complicit in this light betrayal.

Despite their allusions to traversing the boundaries of moral acceptability, the women in these paintings fulfil the archetypes of performer, muse and flirt – in other words, vectors of male pleasure. In this context, the graphic works of Jeanne Mammen offer a startling counterpoint to the overwhelmingly binary male-female offerings by her contemporaries. Schooled in Paris, Mammen returned to Berlin in 1916 where she undertook regular commissions for illustrated magazines on fashion and social satire before her career was curtailed by the censorship of such publications during the Third Reich. Scholarly accounts of her practice portray her as a loner-artist, and yet it should be acknowledged that this solitary status was integral to Mammen's approach. The shifting socio-economic conditions of Weimar Berlin created new possibilities for women in the Republic: as well as subverting expectations of what women could achieve beyond being homemakers and mothers, the changing boundaries of moral acceptability meant that women could inhabit the spaces of the cabarets and bars without the same degree of scrutiny that occurred before the Weimar era.[9] As such, the habit of *flâneur*, to absorb the sights of the city by traversing its streets, as described by writers such as Walter Benjamin, was no longer exclusively a male prerogative.[10]

Mammen's observations of Berlin in the 1920s and the female characters that inhabit it differ significantly from those of her male contemporaries, and give visual expression to female desire and to women's experiences of city life. Her women are frequently stationary and pensive but nonetheless instilled with agency, conveyed through her consistent attention to facial expression. These protagonists often betray their attitude towards other players in the scene, for another distinctive characteristic of Mammen's practice is the contrast between her depictions of women together, and those of women with men. In the latter, the dynamic is usually shown as cool and unaffectionate, as if following obligatory codes of male-female social hierarchies and etiquette. The portraits of women, however, show levels of camaraderie, whether in platonic companionship or in an implied closer, romantic alliance. *Langweilige Puppen* (Boring Dolls) 1929 expresses the

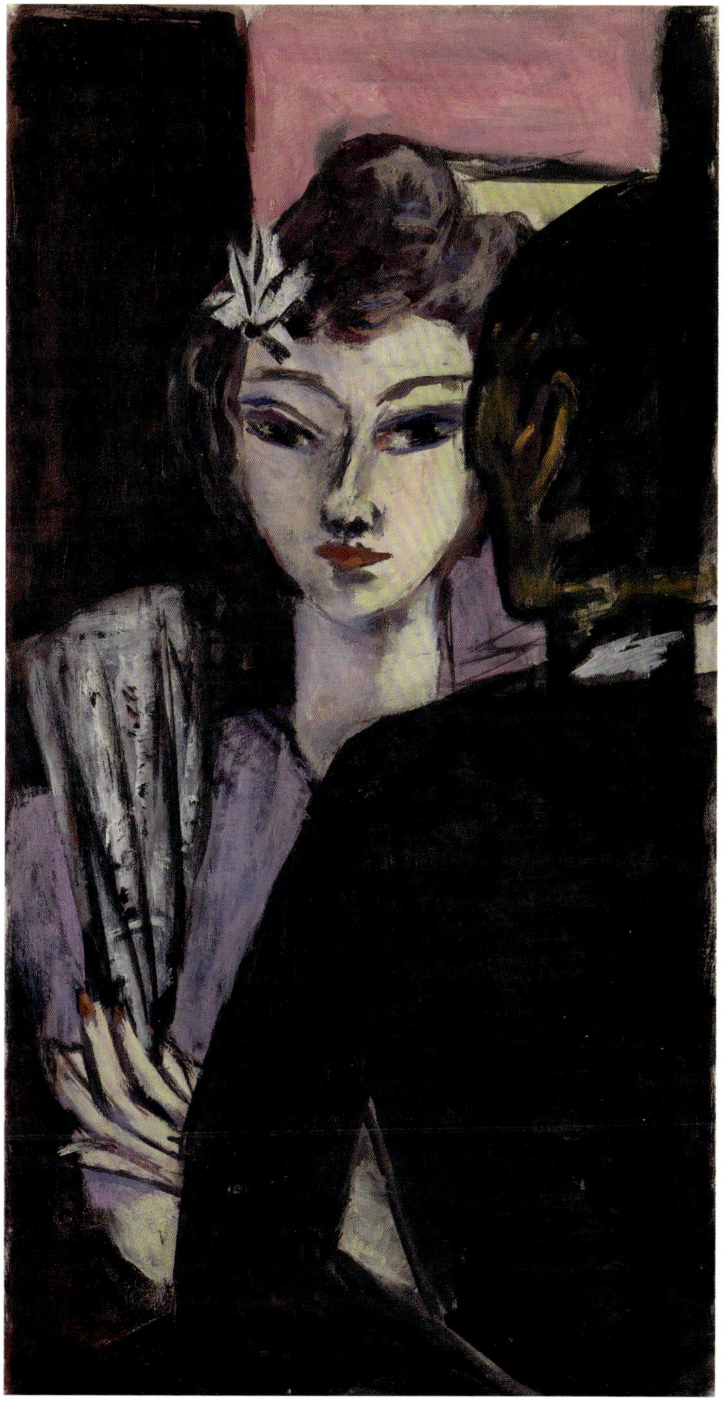

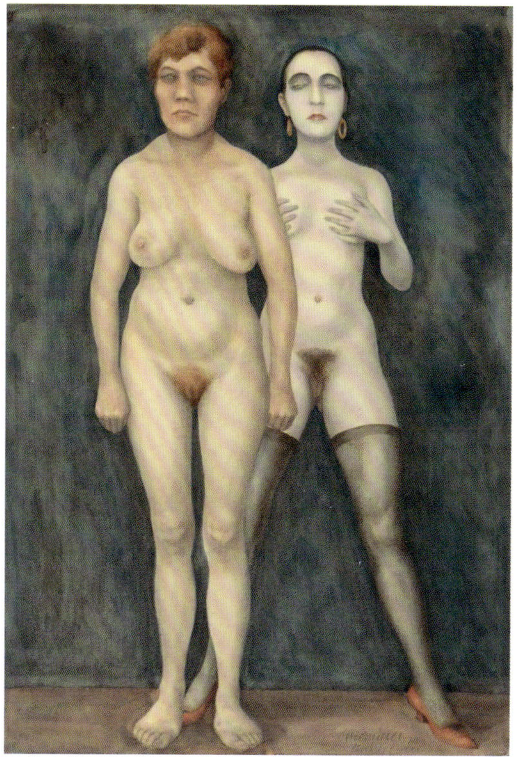

Max Beckmann
Anni (Girl with Fan)
Anni (Mädchen mit Fächer) 1942
Oil paint on canvas
84.6 × 44.5 (left)

Otto Griebel
Two Women
Zwei Frauen 1924
Watercolour on cardboard
63.8 × 45 (above)

ennui of leisure time (p.79). Two slim and fashionable young women, who are immaculately dressed, coiffed and made-up, are shown in what appears to be a domestic setting, their resolutely blank expressions mirroring the costumed doll behind them. Meanwhile, *Brüderstrasse (Zimmer frei)* (Brüderstrasse (Free Room)) 1930 (p.80) depicts three women crowded around an open window. Affixed to the adjacent wall is a sign stating *Zimmer frei* (room available). Despite their cropped hairstyles, their overall appearances do not conform to the fashionable, androgynous garçonne stereotypes. Indeed, the bare flesh and curves might be viewed as showcasing their feminine attributes, with the smirks on their faces indicating a frank acceptance of the drudgery of their occupation. By contrast, *An der Schießbude* (At the Shooting Gallery) 1929 (p.79) reveals a business transaction: as mundane as the fairground is supposed to be thrilling. Judging by the stern expressions of their faces, neither fairground attendant nor patron takes any pleasure in this exchange, which is made all the more disquieting by the conspicuous presentation of a rifle. The juxtaposition between the animated faces of the targets – a Native American, a burlesque act, a soldier and a Grecian muse – serves only to highlight the cool indifference of the human subjects towards each other.

In the context of other depictions of the cabaret and night-time entertainments during the era of the Weimar Republic, Mammen's art serves to complicate our expectations that these spaces were at the ultimate vanguard of social liberalism, and dampens our assumptions that they would be completely unrestrained, outward-looking spaces of tolerance. The interpersonal relationships that she depicts offer a subjective perspective on the world, and the situation of being a solitary woman in Weimar Berlin. While there are evidently allusions to gender subversion in the work of Mammen and her contemporaries, those same works indicate that the dynamics between men and women were still entrenched in social convention. The situations shown by Mammen offer a glimpse into those where desire might not be prescribed or bound by heteronormative conventions, despite the wider context of a society caught between military conflicts, and internally conflicted by attitudes towards gender.

KW

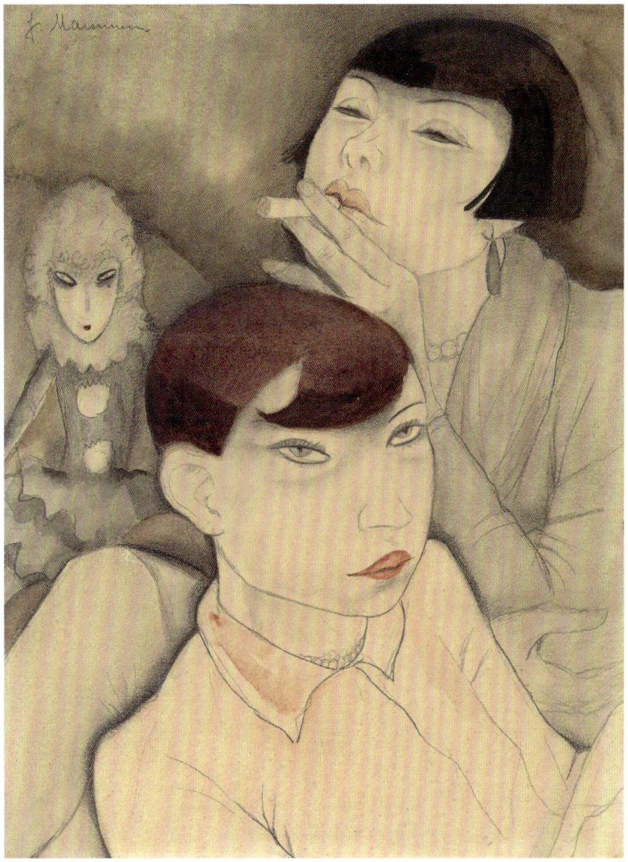

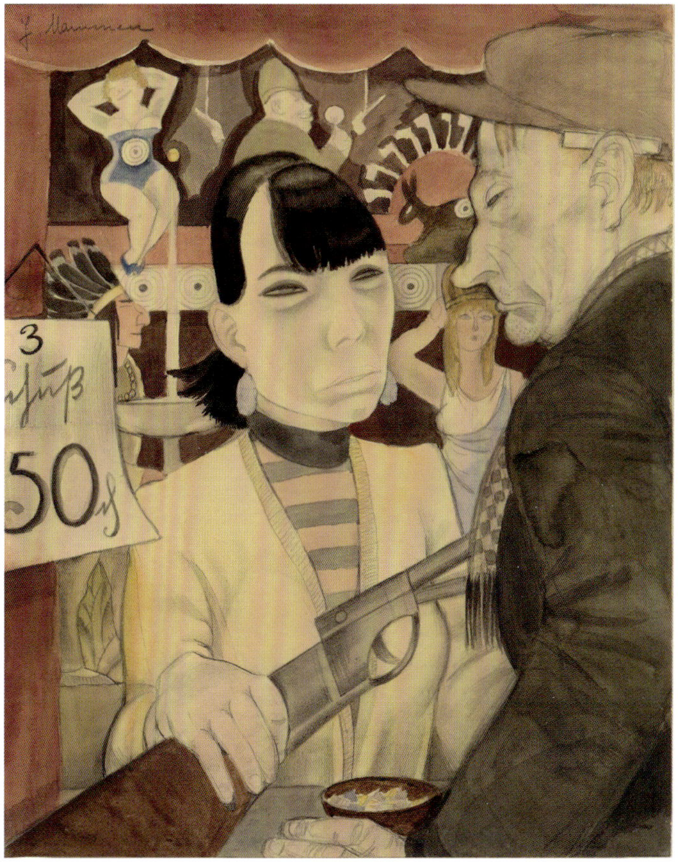

Jeanne Mammen
Boring Dolls
Langweilige Puppen 1929
Watercolour and graphite on
paper mounted on cardboard
38.4 × 28.6

Jeanne Mammen
At the Shooting Gallery
An der Schießbude 1929
Watercolour and graphite on vellum
44.5 × 36

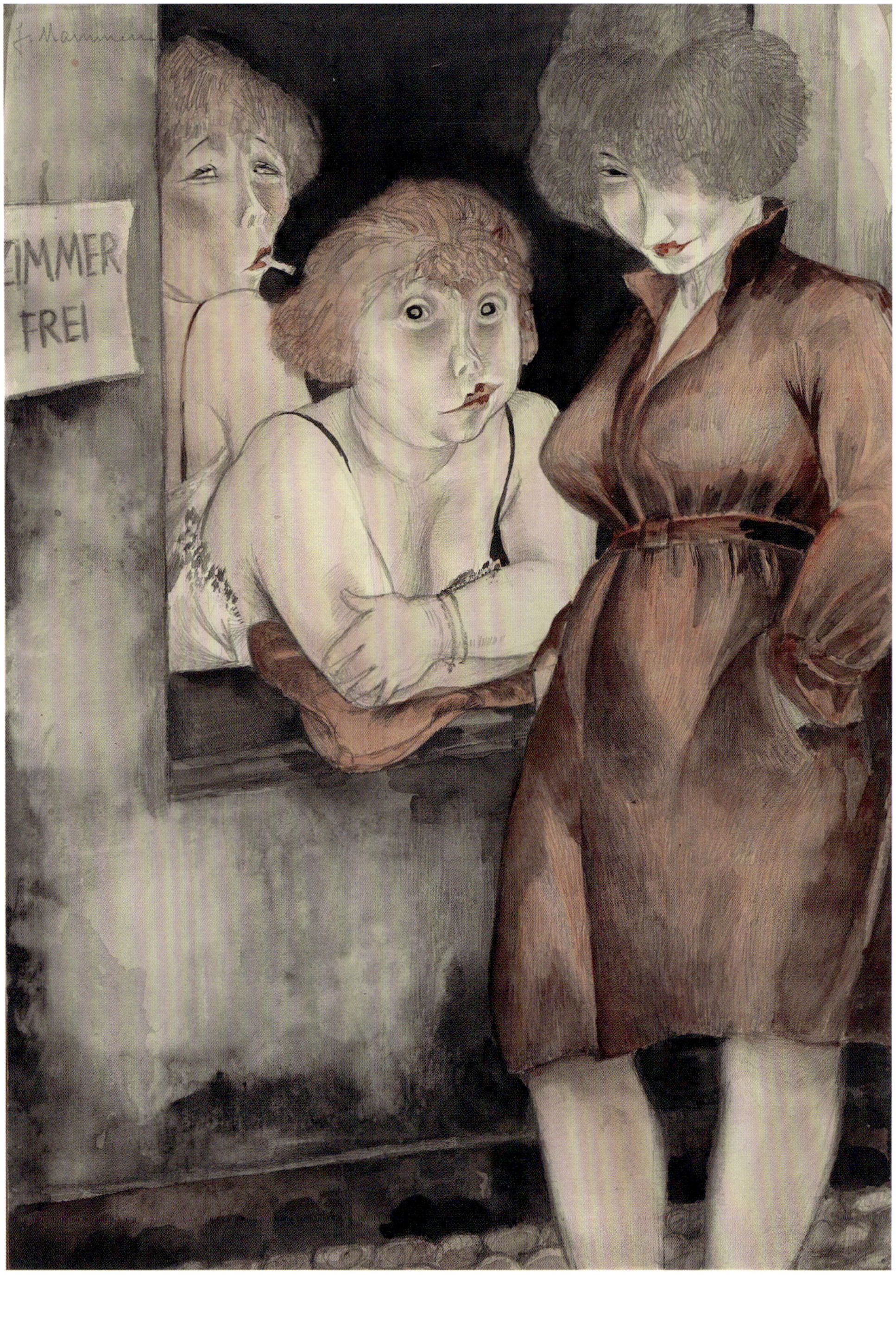

Jeanne Mammen
Brüderstrasse (Free Room)
Brüderstrasse (Zimmer frei) 1930
Watercolour, ink and
graphite on vellum
47.5 × 34.5

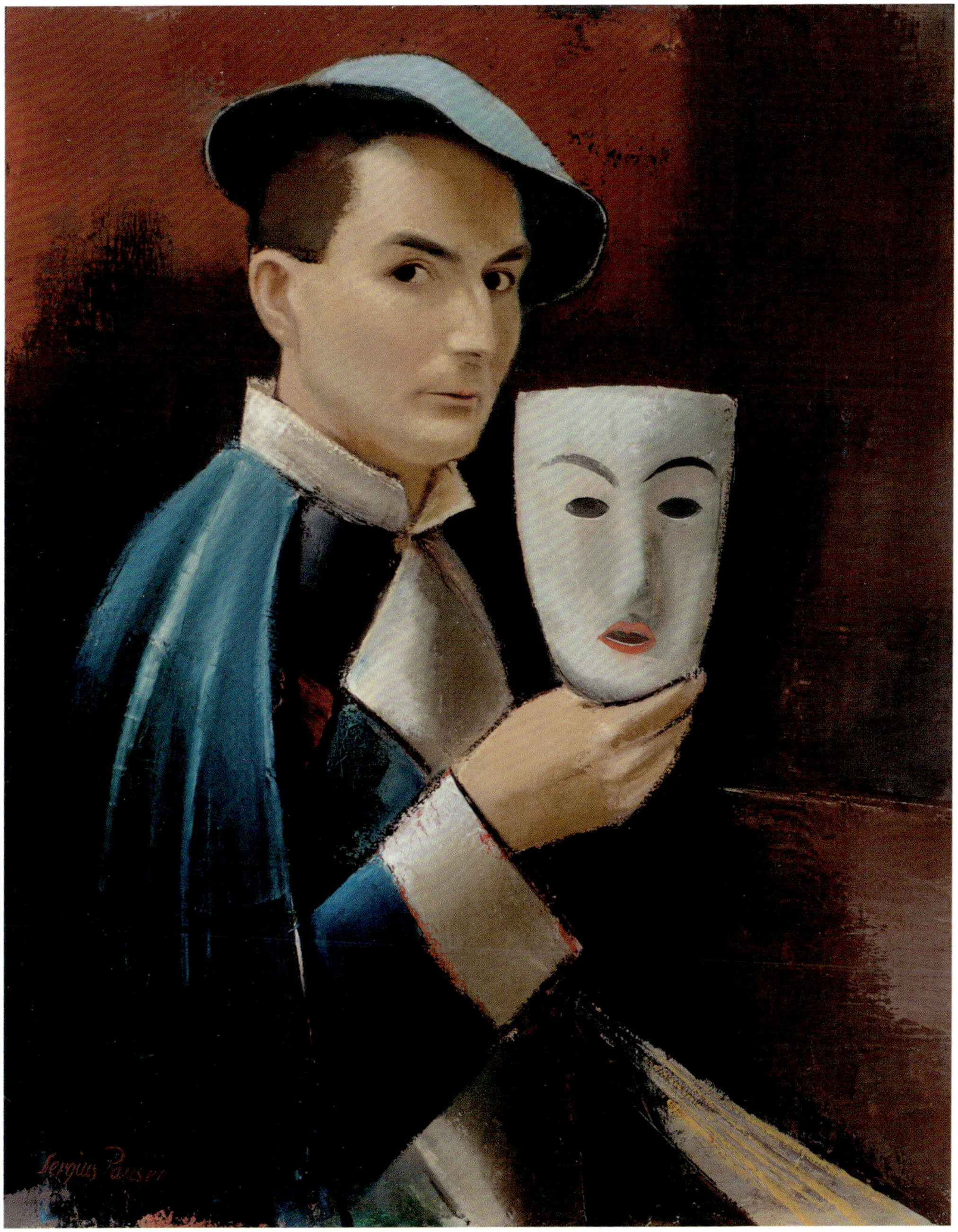

Sergius Pauser
Self-Portrait with Mask
Selbstbildnis mit Maske 1926
Oil paint on canvas
60 × 73

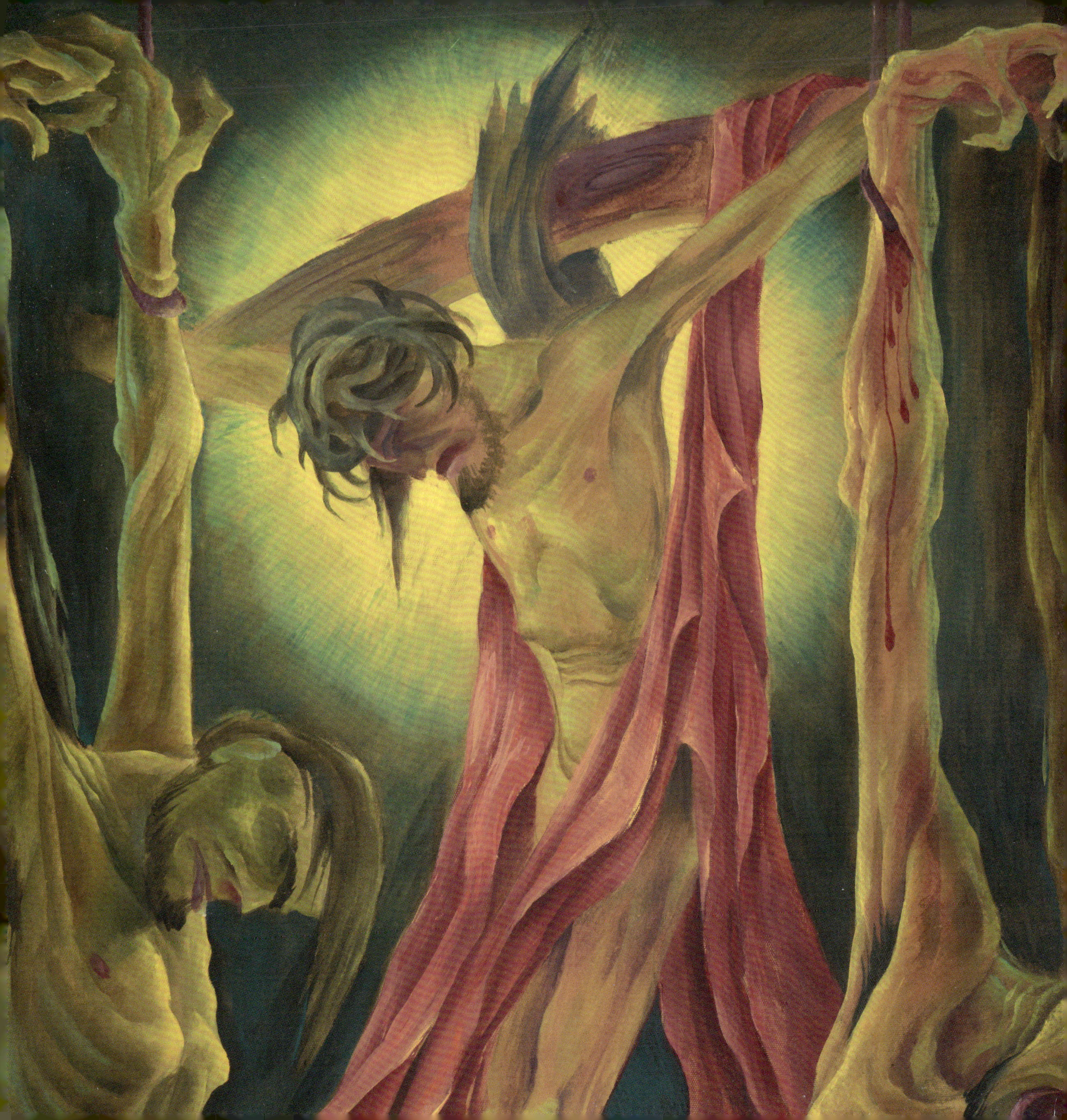

Faith and Magic: 'A Higher Degree of Reality'

In his 1925 book Franz Roh ventured to distinguish the new art as including 'few religious themes'.[1] It may be that his reluctance to dismiss entirely this characteristic (otherwise associated with expressionism) was borne of the memory of the excitement caused by Matthias Grünewald's *Isenheim Altarpiece* c.1512–16 when it was shown in the Pinakothek in Munich. In 1917 the great painting had been moved from wartime Alsace for safety, and, on completion of the conservation work, it went on public display for a year. Dramatically, given Grünewald's extraordinary image of the crucified Christ (pp.84–5), this display began at the moment of Germany's defeat in November 1918 and was concluded only in September 1919.[2] The critic and supporter of expressionism Wilhelm Hausenstein described it at the time as an object of 'pilgrimage', remarking:

> They came. They were drawn to it. The altar was a magnet ... A changed spirit moved, even in the dumb worship of the most wretched. After the mechanisms of more than four years of war, the masses gathered together for the first time before the Spirit of a German artist – probably the greatest we have ever had – to share their innermost common predicament.[3]

The painting remained on view throughout the concurrent revolutionary events at home and peace treaty negotiations abroad. While those sympathetic to the Communist revolutions were agnostic or anti-religious, it is evident that the *Isenheim Altarpiece* answered a spiritual need. The last opportunity to see the altar wings being opened was reported in the newspapers and the painting's return to Colmar (by then in France) on 27 September 1919 was mourned as a loss to German culture equivalent to the territorial loss of Alsace itself.[4] Recognising the compelling power of the image, Hausenstein identified its contemporaneity: 'It could not be otherwise, that the art of our time claimed the altar for itself, as a witness to its rights.'[5]

This communal fascination gave artists access to the rich seam of the German tradition. The anxious visions of Grünewald (and his contemporaries including Albrecht Dürer and Albrecht Altdorfer) gave licence to work that was at once realistic and distorted, imagining religious subjects in a 'verist' style. Among others, such unflinching

Detail, see p.87

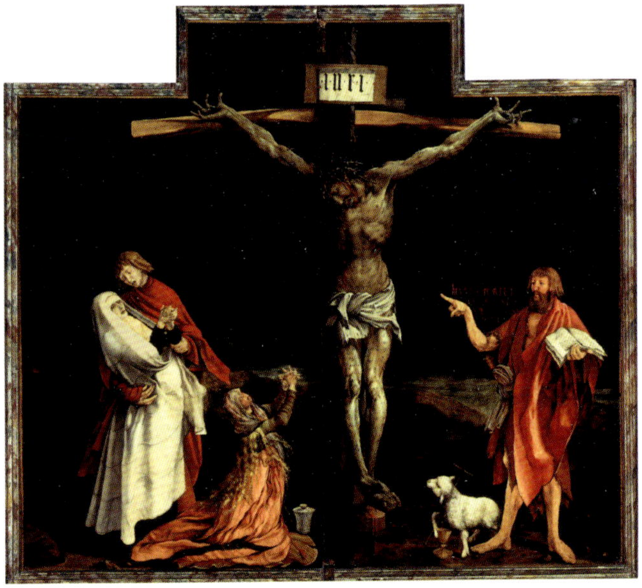

Matthias Grünewald, 1455–c.1528
'Crucifixion' from the Isenheim Altarpiece (closed)
Musée Unterlinden de Colmar

precision so marked Otto Dix's aspiration that he was nicknamed 'Baldung-Dix' after the Renaissance painter Hans Baldung Grien.[6] In this tendency the extreme experiences of the war cast a long shadow and peopled the war memoirs that began to emerge in the late 1920s, a delayed reaction that was common to all combating nations. Memorialisation proved controversial. This was notably the case for Dix's *Schutzengraben* (The Trench) 1920–3 (destroyed) and his later *Der Krieg* (War Triptych) 1932 (Staatliche Kunstsammlungen, Dresden) as well as Ernst Barlach's suspended bronze war memorial, *Der Schwebende* (The Hovering) 1927 in Güstrow Cathedral. By the mid-1920s, war-weary pacifism was evolving into nationalist memory. Dix's detailed depiction of squalor and the melancholy of Barlach's wingless angel, together with Erich Maria Remarque's novel *Im Westen nichts Neues* (All Quiet on the Western Front) of 1928, were all seen by those on the right as insults to the memory of those who had died.[7]

An immediate response to the power of Grünewald is discernible in Albert Birkle's cycle of religious works completed in 1921. *Kreuzigung* (Crucifixion) and *Der Eremit* (The Hermit) (pp.86–7) address explicitly Christian themes and, in a verist vein, take inspiration directly from the searing images of suffering in the *Isenheim Altarpiece*. Birkle imagined etiolated bodies, with Christ in the Crucifixion distinguished from the accompanying good and bad thieves by a yellow-green aura that closely echoes that of Grünewald's *Risen Christ* (p.85). It is not surprising if, in the postwar moment, the pessimism of sacrifice displaced the optimism of resurrection found in the original. Birkle was only twenty-one when he made these paintings, but, having seen active service in the war, the physical distortions may derive from direct experience. His religious imagery, therefore, speaks for personal concerns as well as a wider-held search for spiritual redemption such as Hausenstein had recognised in the response to Grünewald.

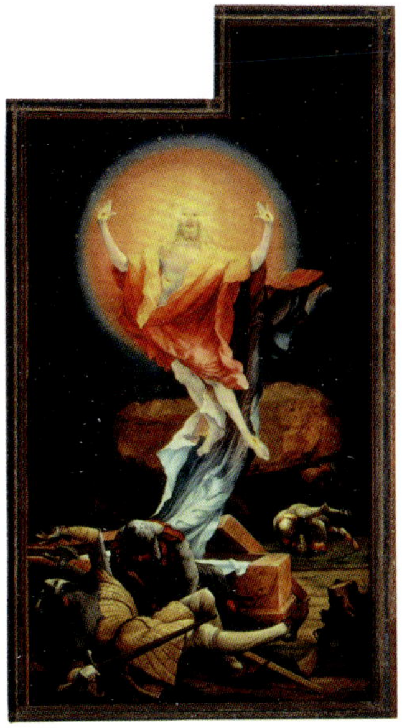

Matthias Grünewald, 1455–c. 1528
'Resurrection' from the Isenheim Altarpiece (right wing)
Musée Unterlinden de Colmar

Herbert Gurschner appears to have been more attuned to Italian Renaissance precedents. This allowed him to achieve a certain calm in images indebted to the sorts of robust figures found in the paintings of Giotto and Paolo Uccello, an enthusiasm shared with his Italian *metafisica* contemporaries. When his *Verkündigung* (The Annunciation) 1929–30 (p.89) was shown in London in 1931, J.B. Manson, the then director of the Tate Gallery, claimed: 'It can hold its own with distinction even among those early paintings when the subject had a spiritual significance for painters, profounder than any it can have for the artists of to-day.'[8] An undertow of anxiety came to the surface, however, in *Triumph des Todes* (Triumph of Death) 1927 and *Lazarus* 1928 (pp.92–3). In both, the painter uses a centralising composition to gather a crowd of figures that establishes a claustrophobic atmosphere. The former painting draws on a long tradition of confronting the inevitability of mortality, while the latter is centred on the frigid body of the resurrected believer, its morbidity conveying a sense of horror as much as hope. Although more active in Britain as the 1930s drew on, Gurschner's roots in the Tyrol presented a particular context allowing him to draw upon pictorial traditions from both sides of the Alps.[9] While the imagery may be read as conservative, this conciliatory position may be seen as part of the dialogue with the Italian tradition that also concerned Theodor Däubler and Roh.

Beyond orthodox Christianity a number of turn-of-the-century mystical, esoteric and hermetic beliefs regained popularity during and after the war. These ranged from the influence of theosophy and Rudolf Steiner's Anthroposophical Society to the admiration for the spiritual creativity of Rabindranath Tagore promoted on his lecture tours of Germany in the 1920s.[10] In pursuit of the 'total artwork', Johannes Itten infused his teaching at the Bauhaus with his commitment to the Zoroastrian religion of Mazdaznan.[11] Heinrich Maria Davringhausen's *Der Dichter Däubler* (The Poet Däubler) 1917 (p.11) appears to make manifest some of these spiritual concerns. Hieratic and dominant, the poet is shown dressed in orange and with trance-like staring eyes. He towers over a night-time landscape that is eerily lit by cosmic signs.[12] This serves as a visual equivalent of Däubler's

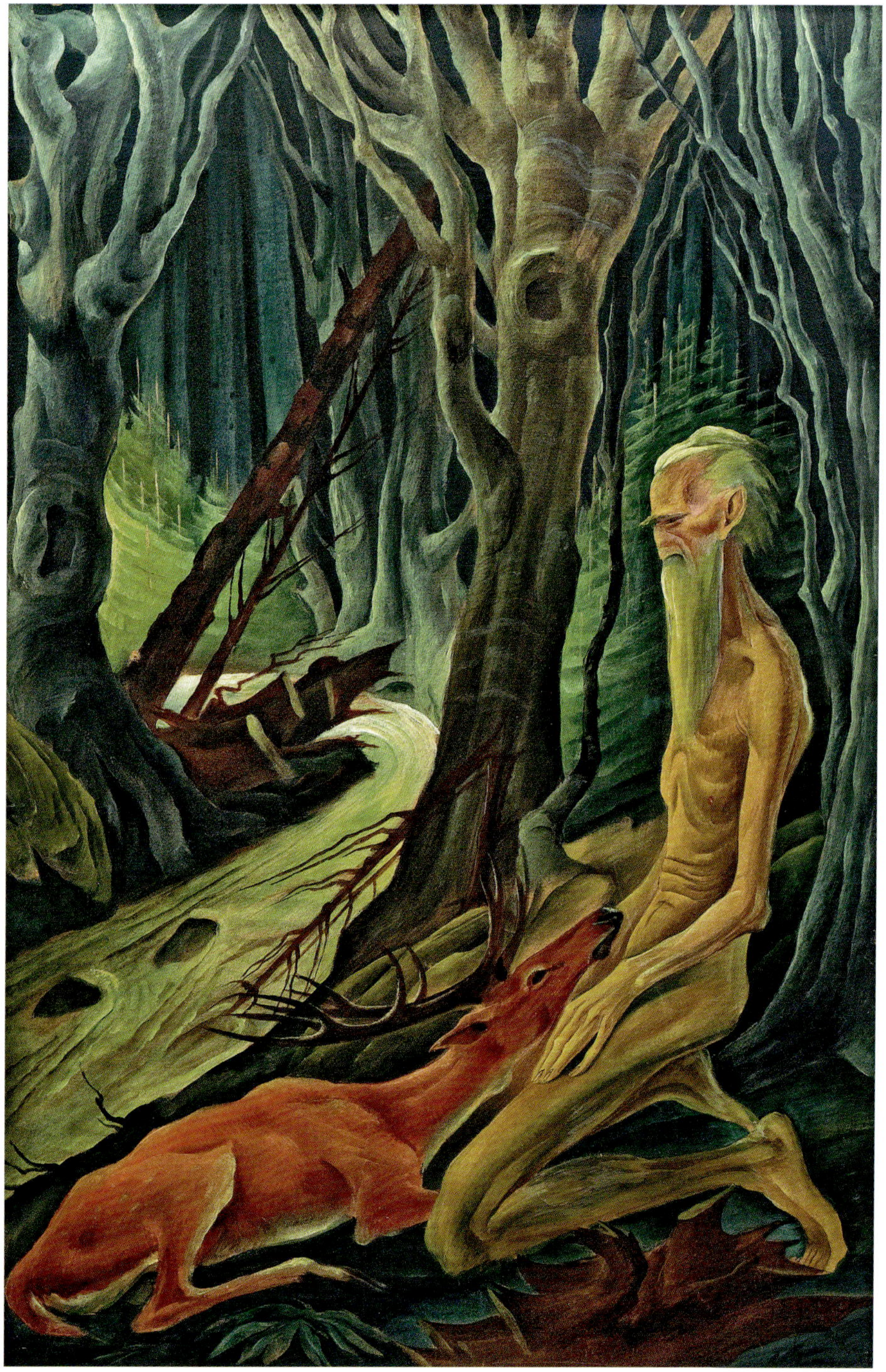

Albert Birkle
The Hermit
Die Eremit 1921
Oil paint on canvas
91 × 60.5

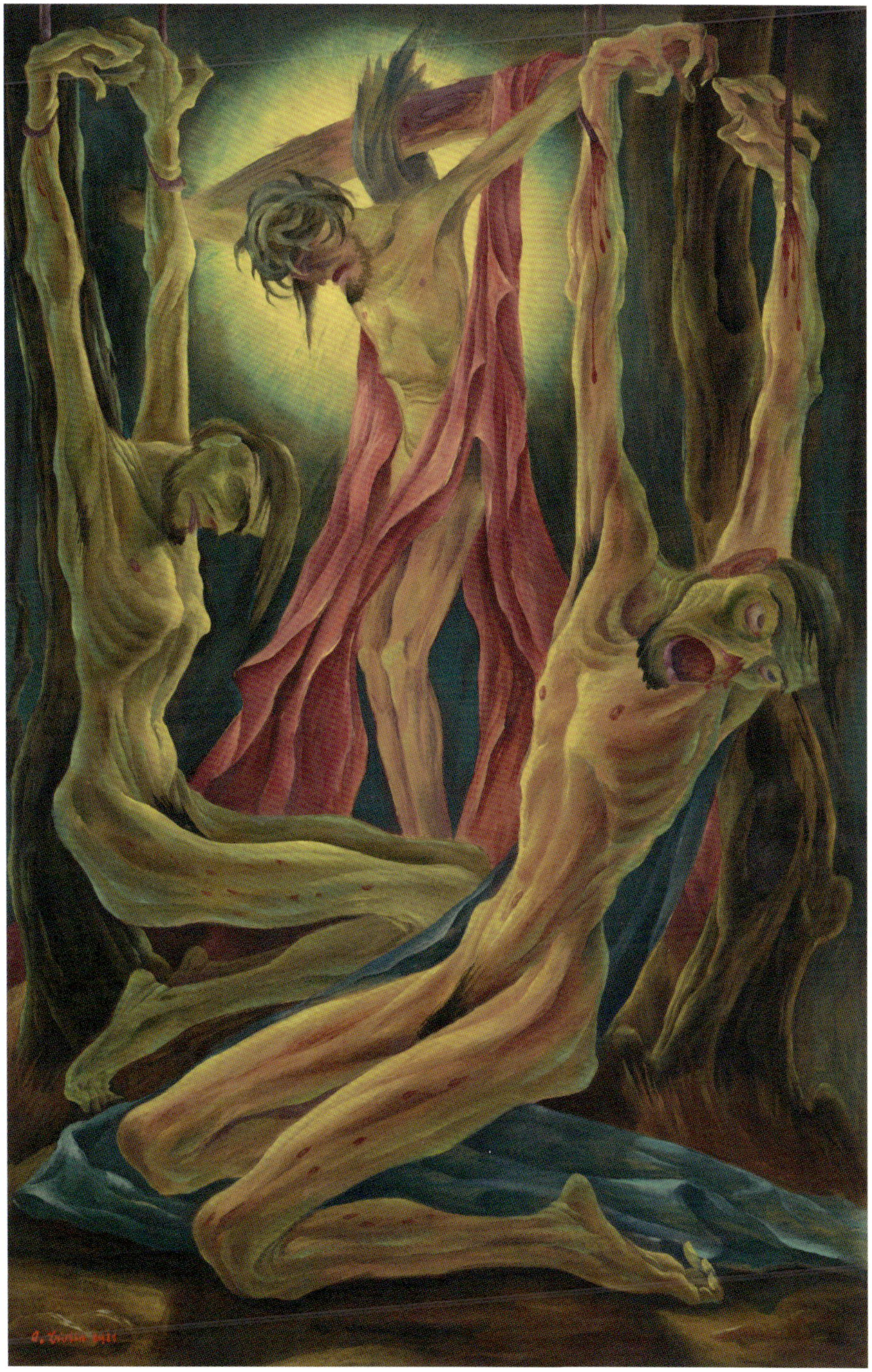

Albert Birkle
Crucifixion
Kreuzigung 1921
Oil paint on board
92 × 60.7

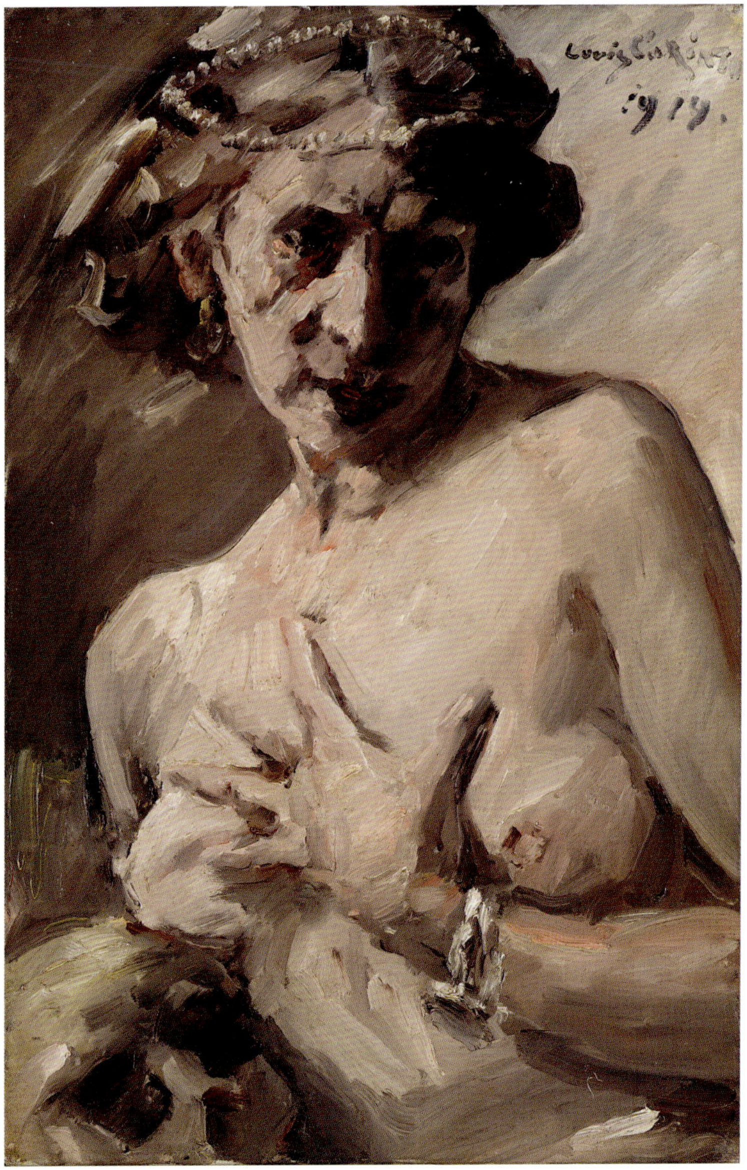

Lovis Corinth
Magdalen with Pearls in her Hair
Magdalena mit Perlenkette im Haar 1919
Oil paint on canvas
71.5 × 47.6

Opposite page:
Herbert Gurschner
The Annunciation
Verkündigung 1929–30
Oil paint on canvas
161.7 × 191.1

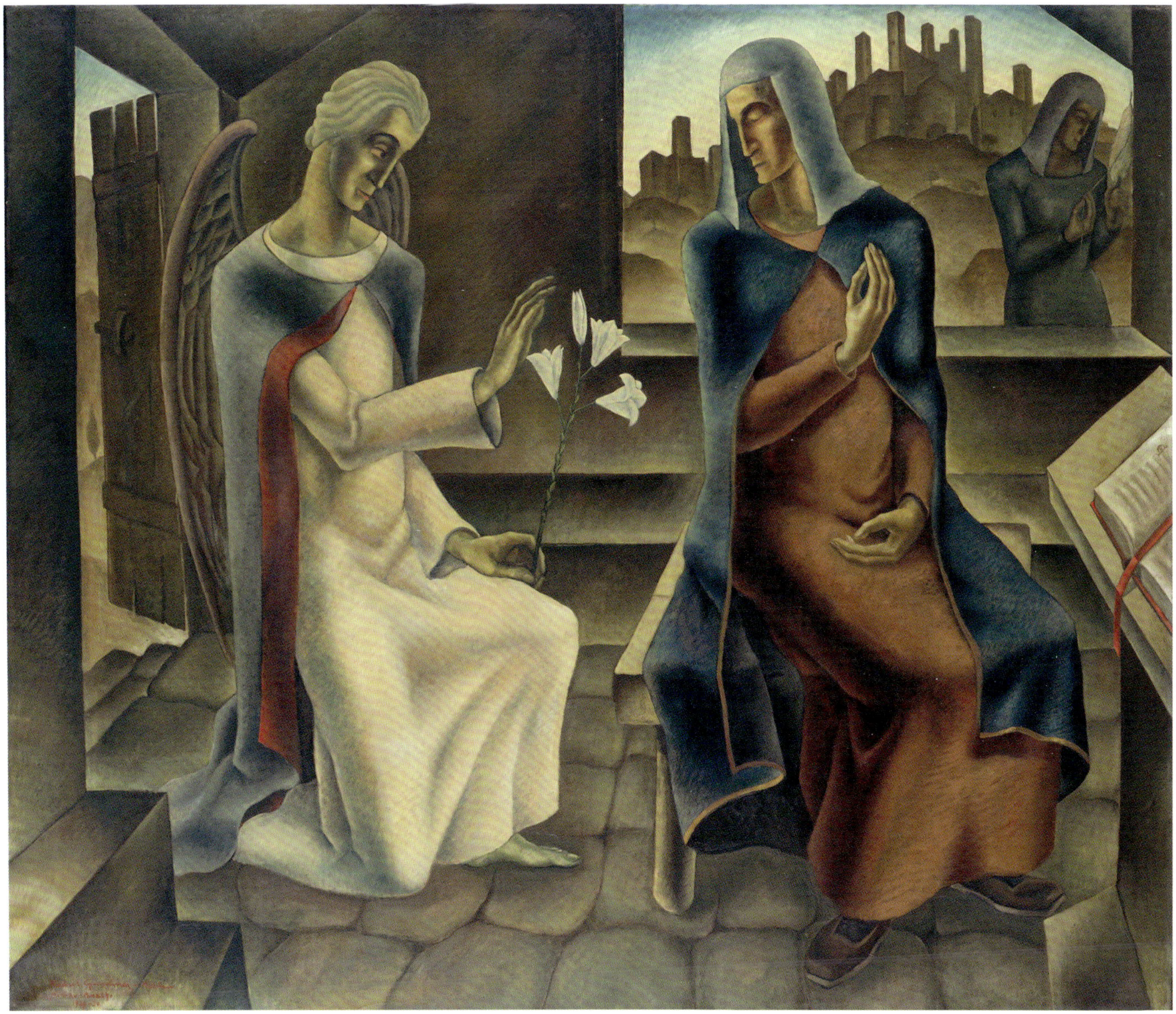

epic poem *Das Nordlicht* (The Northern Lights/Aurora Borealis), published in 1921 after a decade of gestation, that includes memories of Italy and Greece evoked through visionary verses.[13] To some degree *Das Nordlicht* has parallels with the exactly contemporary *Duino Elegies* on which Rainer Maria Rilke had also been working for the decade that straddled the war.[14] The final Elegy, completed in 1921, begins ecstatically: 'Some day, emerging at last from this terrifying vision, / May I burst into jubilant praise to assenting Angels!'[15] Rilke imagined his angel as a higher being associated with 'a higher degree of reality in the invisible',[16] and there is an aspect of a spiritual guide that echoes Beatrice's role in Dante's *Divine Comedy* (c.1308–20). Between the well-established Rilke and the itinerant Däubler a shared sense of the currency of visionary experience is readily traceable.

It is a measure of the complexity of the tendencies that can be gathered under the umbrella of magic realism that the visionary and the precise could be maintained side by side. It suggests that the otherworldly was, for some, as present as the material world intent on reconstruction and industrialisation. Even in one of the most apparently factual of portraits, Rudolf Schlichter's *Lady with Red Scarf (Speedy with the Moon)* 1933 (p.67), the insistent presence of the individual is accompanied by contrasting cosmological signs in the sky beyond. Through the precision of this juxtaposition, Schlichter offers an equivalence between the two realms. In the early 1920s he had been close to George Grosz and to Berlin dada, offering a critique of the status quo.[17] This portrait was painted in the critical year that the National Socialists consolidated their power in the country with Hitler's appointment as chancellor. Although Schlichter's politics had shifted towards religious, and even nationalist, sentiments, the cosmic setting for this portrait suggests the foreboding with which many greeted the precipitous political change.

The assessment of the deeper meaning of the work associated with magic realism and *Neue Sachlichkeit* could differ widely even – perhaps especially – among those commentators who were most closely involved. Just as Roh was inclined to confine religious themes to the older generation of visionary expressionism, so Gustav Friedrich Hartlaub could not attribute any spiritual qualities to the new art. 'Cynicism and resignation are the negative side of the Neue Sachlichkeit', he told Alfred H. Barr Jr, the director of New York's Museum of Modern Art, in 1929, while adding, 'the positive

He was just considering this strange transformation when music resounded. Initially, it reminded him of his hurdy-gurdy. But then the sounds swelled, they flowed and poured and broadened; collapsed again, began to whisper, removed themselves, and then turned back. The room was full of people. They knelt down. The candles on either side of the cross burned with golden flames and spread a fragrance of incenses and stearin. With that, Andreas understood that he had died, and was standing before the Heavenly Judge. Nor was he a boy anymore either. He was the only person standing among a thousand kneeling in the whole room. He took a step forward on his crutch, but it made no sound. Andreas saw that he was standing on soft clouds. He remembered the speech that he had prepared for the earthly hearing. A powerful anger welled up in him, his complexion reddened, and his soul gave birth to words, angry purple words, a thousand, ten thousand, a million words. They were not words that he had ever heard or thought or read. They had slept deep within him, tamed by his miserable intellect, atrophied under the cruel veneer of his life. Now they sprouted and fell from him like blossoms from a tree. The solemn and mournful music continued softly in the background. Andreas heard it as he listened to the roaring of his own speech. I have awakened from my servile meekness into red, rebellious obstinacy. I would deny You, God, if I were alive and not standing before You. But seeing You with my own eyes and hearing You with my own ears, I must do worse than deny You: I must revile You!

Joseph Roth, *Die Rebellion*, Berlin 1924, as *Rebellion*, translated by Michael Hofmann, London 1999, pp.140–1

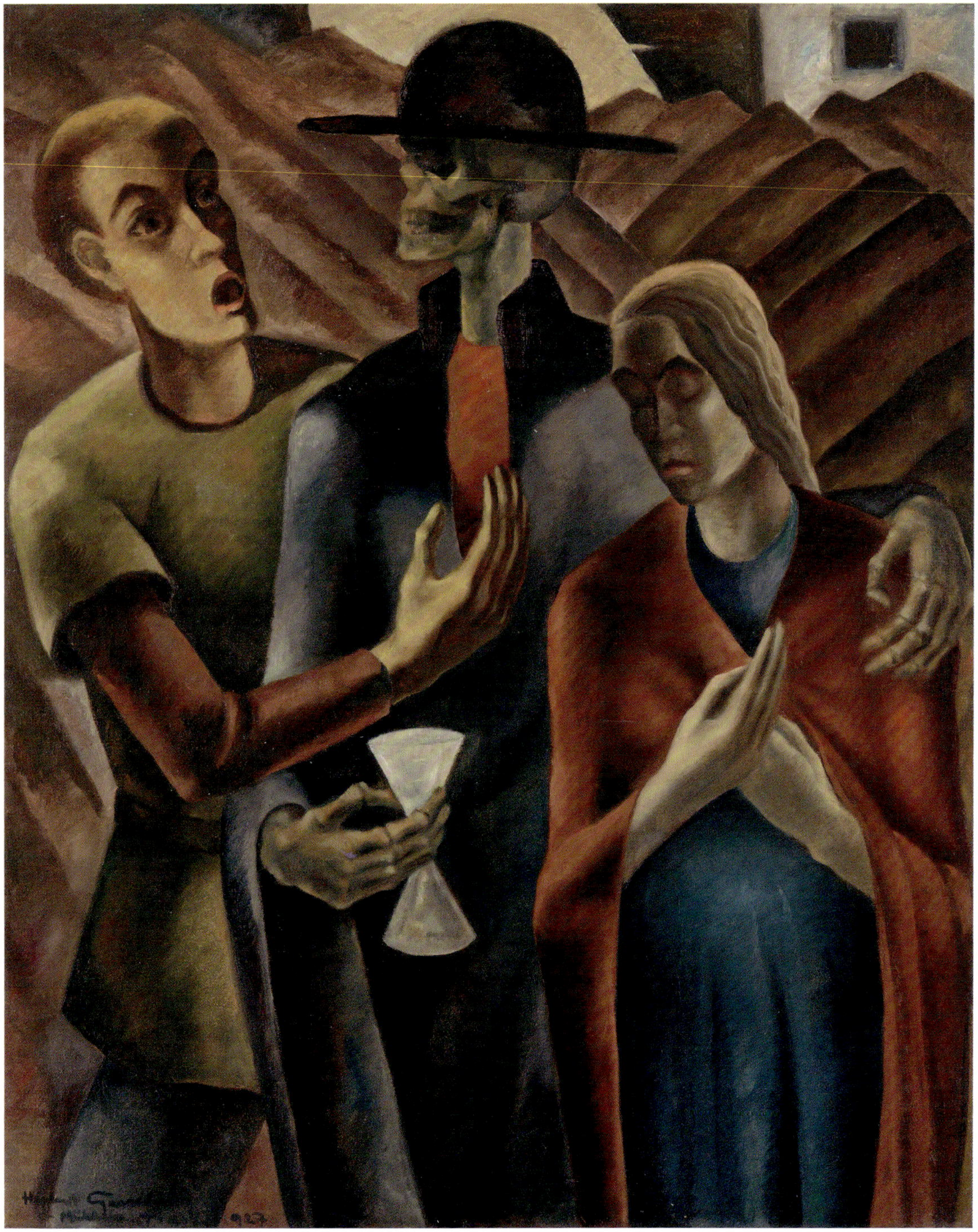

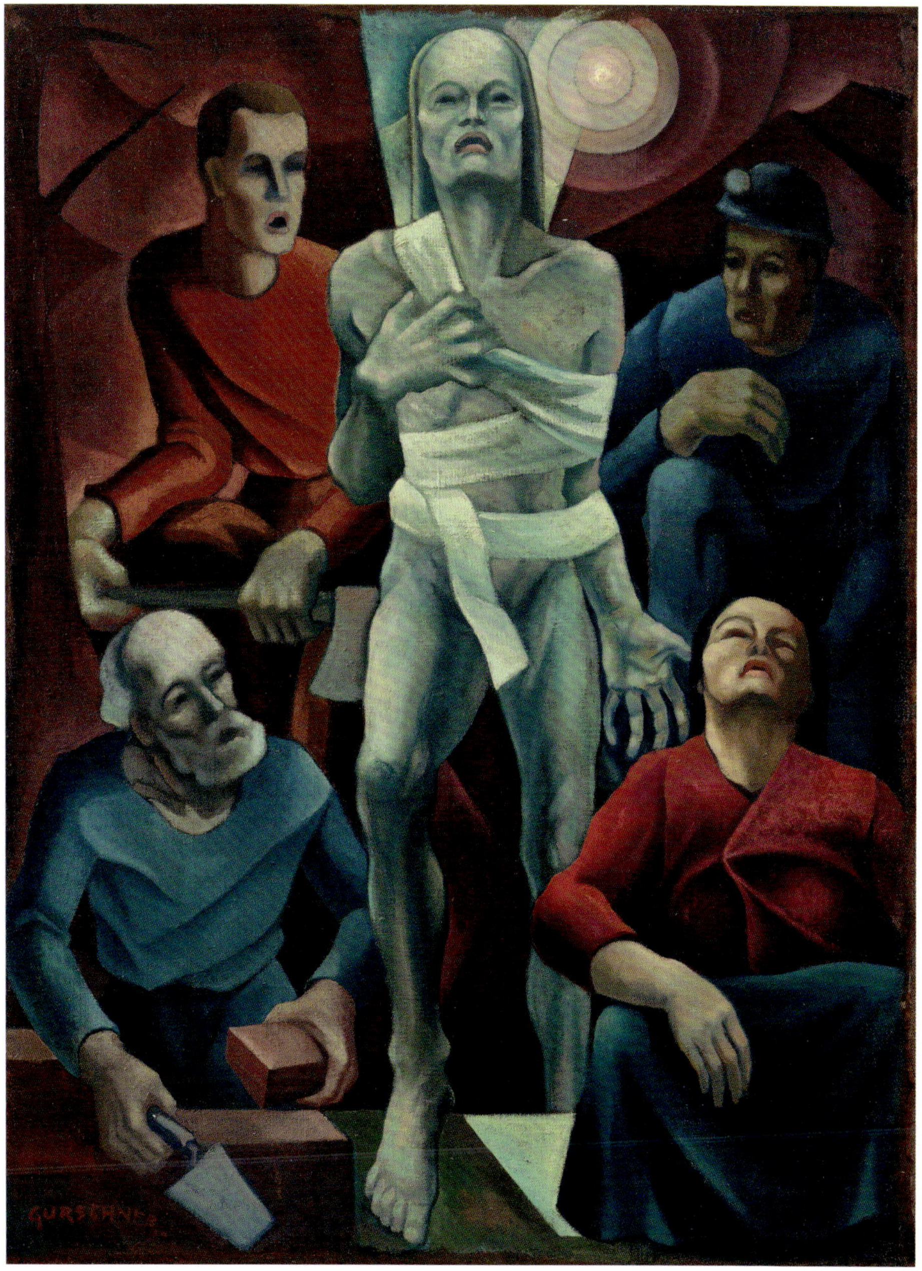

Opposite page:
Herbert Gurschner
Triumph of Death
Triumph des Todes 1927
Oil paint on canvas
109 × 89.5

Herbert Gurschner
Lazarus (The Workers)
Lazarus (Die Arbeiter) 1928
Oil paint on canvas
92 × 69

side expresses itself in the immediate reality as a result of the desire to take things entirely objectively on a material basis without immediately investing them with ideal implication.'[18] By emphasising the objective and the cynical, he reaffirmed the particular position that had underpinned his exhibition four years earlier. At least one critic, Misch Orend, saw the worth of Roh's term within a longer view. Transforming the emphasis on objectivity, he wrote: 'This new magic is the visible existence of the things themselves as they preserve it in themselves without reference to the human world. It is their uniqueness – and therefore infinity – with the uncanny calm that surrounds them.'[19] In this respect the presence (and presentation) of objects within, but outside, human control was positioned as a dispassionate observation of an independent 'other' stripped to essentials so as to be at once uncanny in its 'unqualified autonomy' and both 'tragic and serious'. It is not surprising that Grosz epitomised the cynicism that Hartlaub had observed. Writing in 1931, the artist proclaimed: 'in this faithless and materialistic time one should use paper and slate to show people the devilish mug concealed in their own faces. Let us tear down the storehouse of ready-mades and all the manufactured junk and show the ghostly nothing behind them.'[20]

While these debates were overtaken by the political turning point of 1933, a decade later Lea Grundig made her allegorical drawing *In den Abgrund* (Into the Abyss) 1943 (p.95), while, coincidentally, Thomas Mann began to write *Doctor Faustus* (published 1947). Grundig conjured an apocalyptic vision with explicit reference to the Holocaust, as a knot of naked figures suspended in a tenebrous space struggle to salvage those falling about them. This might be the heartrending scene witnessed by the 'angel of history' backing into the future that Walter Benjamin imagined when considering Paul Klee's *Angelus Novus* 1920.[21] Mann's fictive biography of the imagined composer Adrian Leverkühn also surveyed the wreckage of the recent past. Although announced in the familiarity of the fable, the composer's final, bilious confession that he had made a pact with the devil is achieved in such a way as to transform the novel's retracing of the fervid atmosphere of the Weimar Republic.[22] Embedded in the longer trajectory of German culture, these contrasting accounts reflect on the hope and compromises of the 1920s, which, however liberal in its values, provided the fertile ground for their total destruction.

MG

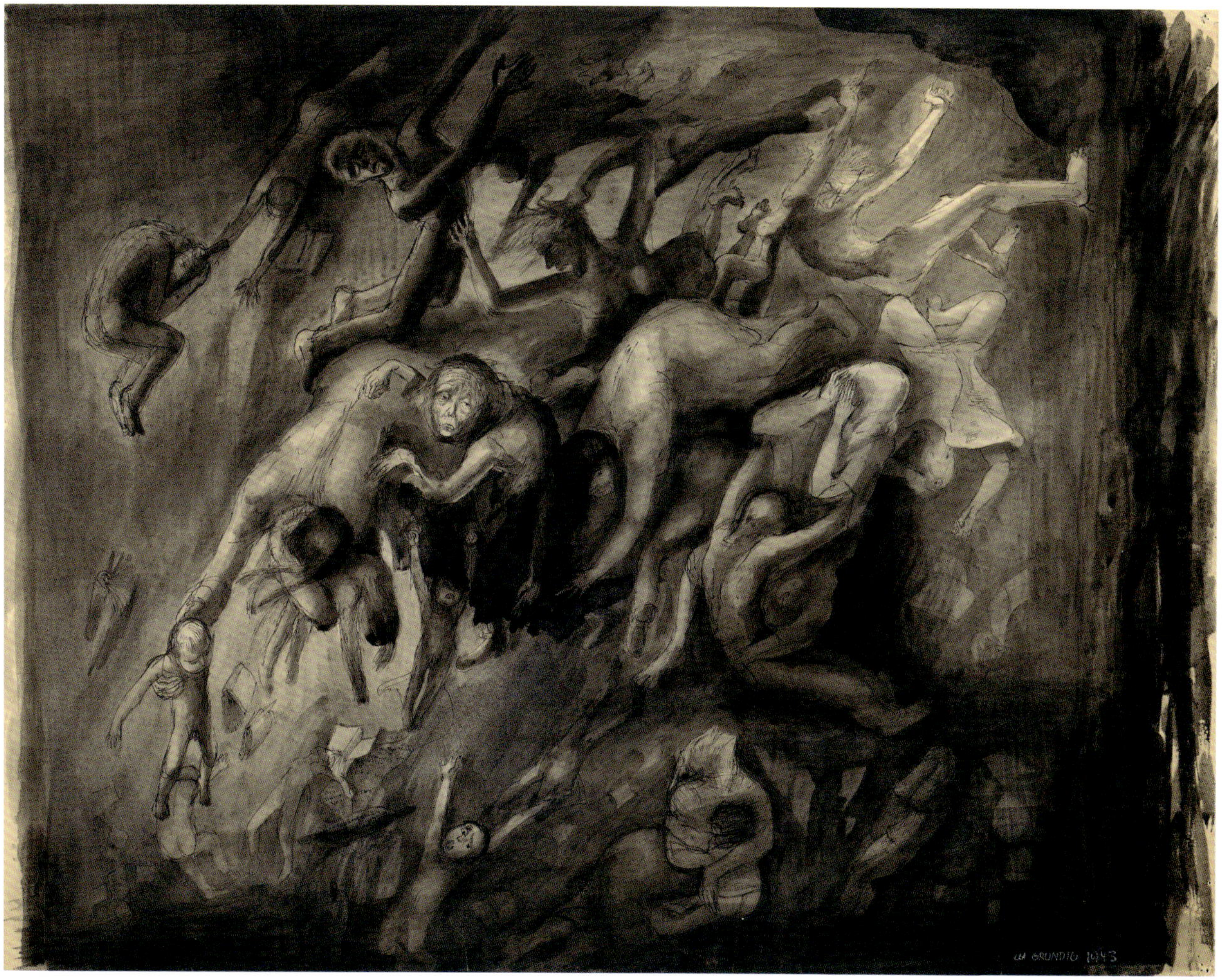

Lea Grundig
Into the Abyss
In den Abgrund 1943
Pen and ink on cardboard
44 × 56

Coda: ‘From the Visible to the Invisible’

Realism in painting was an ideological battleground in the mid-1930s. Its various modes reflected the political divide but also revealed propagandising practices common to the rival totalitarian regimes in Europe. In Germany, by September 1933, the National Socialists had enforced their racially determined view of culture by sacking socialists and Jews associated with modernism, and then bringing arts and propaganda under Joseph Goebbels’ single *Reichskulturkammer*. Only a year later, in the following August, Andrei Zhdanov established socialist realism at the First All-Union Congress of Soviet Writers in Moscow as the only acceptable style to ‘depict reality in its revolutionary development’.[1] This was elaborated by Karl Radek who declared: ‘Realism ... means reflecting reality as it is, in all its complexity, in all its contrariety, and not only capitalist reality, but also that other, new reality – the reality of socialism.’[2] Both positions were to result in a realism in which heroising celebration displaced any critical reflection on actuality, let alone any sense of cynicism. It is hardly surprising that, while lamenting the state of German repression, the British critic Herbert Read quoted Radek in order to expose the contradiction in determining realism as ideologically defined.[3]

By the summer of 1936, with the German remilitarisation of the Rhineland (March), the Italian victory in Ethiopia (June) and the rebellion, in July, of General Franco against the Spanish Republican government, Read summarised the polarised cultural climate in Europe. ‘It is the presumption of modern dictatorships’, he commented, ‘to challenge in a most direct manner the artist’s creative freedom.’[4] As if in repost, the National Socialists’ *Entartete Kunst* exhibition in Munich in 1937 brought to a climax a wave of anti-modernism. In an echo of Soviet policy that followed equally anti-elitist sentiments, Adolf Hitler declared that ‘the artist creates not for artists but, exactly like everybody else, for the People!’[5] Finding his own work included in the exhibition Max Beckmann left the following day for exile in Amsterdam. He guardedly identified the move towards ‘collectivism’ as the cultural threat from officialdom. In his 1938 speech ‘On My Painting’, Beckmann remarked on this phenomenon (perhaps picturing the propensity for mass parades): ‘Everywhere attempts are being made to lower the happiness and the way of living of mankind to the level of termites.’[6] Both Read and Beckmann were commenting in relation to exhibitions at the New Burlington

Galleries in London: the *International Exhibition of Surrealism* (June–July 1936) and *Twentieth Century German Art* (July–August 1938).

Debate could only be raised abroad – in France and Britain – as restrictions were enforced in Germany. In Paris, the ideological debate was informed by the belief among left-wing intellectuals that the USSR was the only possible bulwark against Fascist Italy, Nazi Germany and their support for Francoist Spain. The former surrealist Louis Aragon led a series of 'Querelles du réalisme' (disputes around realism) at the Communist-run Maison de la Culture in May and June 1936, which were necessarily framed by the doctrine of socialist realism.[7] Acknowledging that modernist artists 'are on the whole hostile to realism', Aragon nevertheless invited the audience to oppose Nazism, 'the real enemy who takes down yesterday's works of art from the walls of the museums, sells them at public auction and burns them with books in the market place'.[8] Alongside Fernand Léger, the architect Le Corbusier took part in the discussion on 31 May and, perhaps because it was most concerned with abstract art, his contribution appeared in the London publication *Circle*. While implying the need to surpass realism with any links to past models, he drew an optimistic conclusion about the state of culture once 'people stop looking behind them and leaning on the Renaissance … but instead go forward to construct something whole and entire'.[9]

For his part, Beckmann remained understandably pessimistic. Even as he knew that the truth-telling associated with realism was unacceptable to those in power, he told his London audience in 1938: 'What I want to show in my work is the idea which hides itself behind so-called reality. I am seeking for the bridge which leads from the visible to the invisible.'[10] More than a decade after Franz Roh and Gustav Friedrich Hartlaub had recognised the cogency of a new tendency, Beckmann thereby restated the fundamental uncanniness of magic realism.

MG

CHRONOLOGY

1914

August: Outbreak of the 'Great War' between Germany and Austria-Hungary ranged against Russia, France, Belgium and Britain.

Among the artists subsequently associated with magic realism who were soon under arms were Max Beckmann, Albert Birkle, Otto Dix, Carl Grossberg, George Grosz and Alexander Kanoldt.

1915

May: Italy declares war on Austria-Hungary. The Austrians defeat the Russians at Lemburg (June); Battle of Ypres on the Western Front.

1916

February–December: Battle of Verdun and Battle of the Somme.
November: Death of Emperor Franz Joseph of Austria-Hungary, ending a sixty-eight-year reign.

February: Foundation of dada at Cabaret Voltaire in Zurich. Christian Schad is linked to dada activities in Geneva.

Max Beckmann suffers a nervous breakdown at the Front. Jeanne Mammen settles in Berlin. Heinrich Harry Deierling and Rudolf Schlichter are called up.

Publication of Franz Kafka's *Die Verwandlung* (Metamorphosis) and Theodor Däubler's *Der neue Standpunkt* (The New Point of View).

1917

April: United States enters the war.

July–November: Third Battle of Ypres (Passchendaele) on the Western Front.

October: The Bolshevik Revolution results in Russian withdrawal from the war.

Heinrich Maria Davringhausen settles in Berlin. George Grosz suffers a nervous breakdown at the Front and returns to Berlin.

Publication of Ivan Goll's *Requiem: Fur die Gefallenen Europas* (Requiem: For Europe's Fallen).

1918

November: Mutinies in the German fleet lead to the November Revolution, the abdication of Kaiser Wilhelm II, the proclamation of the Weimar Republic, and the Armistice that ends the war (11 November). An influenza epidemic kills millions.

New European nations are established: Latvia, Lithuania, Estonia, Poland, Czechoslovakia and Yugoslavia. Civil war in Russia.

Richard Huelsenbeck launches dada in Berlin with Raoul Hausmann and Hannah Höch; Wieland Herzfelde, his brother John Heartfield and George Grosz are key participants.

Foundation of *Arbeitsrat für Kunst* (Working Council for the Arts) led by architects Bruno Taut and Walter Gropius, and the *Novembergruppe* of artists formed by Max Pechstein and others (December).

Heinrich Maria Davringhausen moves to Munich and meets Carlo Mense and Georg Schrimpf, and the art historian Franz Roh.

Publication of Oswald Spengler's *Der Untergang des Abendlandes* (The Decline of the West).

1919

January: The Communist Spartakist uprising in Berlin and Munich, followed by the murder of Communist leaders Karl Liebknecht and Rosa Luxemburg.

April: The revolutionary Räterepublik in Munich, led by Ernst Toller, is violently overthrown by the military (1–2 May). The postwar Treaty of Versailles imposes punitive payments of reparations on Germany, the return of Alsace-Lorraine to France and demilitarisation of the Rhineland.

Foundation of the Bauhaus at Weimar under Walter Gropius, who appoints Johannes Itten as a Bauhaus Master; Carl Grossberg enrols.

Dada activities in Cologne led by Jean (Hans) Arp and Max Ernst, and involving Angelika and Heinrich Hoerle and Franz Wilhelm Seiwert.

Heinrich Maria Davringhausen's exhibition at the Galerie Neue Kunst Hans Goltz, Munich (April). Otto Dix enrols at the Dresden Art Academy and founds the Dresdner Sezession Gruppe (Dresden Secession) with Conrad Felixmüller; with Otto Griebel, they are sympathetic to dada and communism.

Jeanne Mammen settles on the Kurfürstendamm in Berlin. Rudolf Schlichter moves to Berlin and is associated with dada.

Publication of Karl Kraus's *Die letzten Tage der Menschheit* (The Last Days of Mankind), and Franz Werfel's *Der Gerichtstag* (Judgement Day).

1920

The right-wing Kapp Putsch is thwarted in Berlin (March). Spartakist uprising in Ruhr.

Erste Internationale Dada-Messe (First International Dada Fair) in Berlin (June); George Grosz and Rudolf Schlichter are among those prosecuted for insulting the army.

Paul Klee exhibition at the Galerie Neue Kunst Hans Goltz in Munich (May–June).

In *Tribune der Kunst und Zeit*, Kasimir Edschmid publishes 'Creative Confessions', including contributions from Max Beckmann, Conrad Felixmüller and Paul Klee.

In Cologne Heinrich Hoerle and Franz Wilhelm Seiwert form the Kölner Gruppe Progressiver Künstler (Cologne Group of Progressive Artists).

Robert Weine's film, *Das Cabinet des Dr Caligari* (The Cabinet of Dr Caligari) is premiered.

1921

Reparations payments are set at 2 billion gold marks per year. Germany begins to print money to meet the bill, rapidly increasing inflation.

Paul Klee joins the Bauhaus staff.

Berlin prosecution of Wieland Herzfelde and George Grosz for the satirical portfolio using the military motto *Gott mit uns* (God be with us).

Max Beckmann exhibition at the Frankfurter Kunstverein.

Exhibition of Italian *Valori plastici* artists at the Nationalgalerie, Berlin (April). Rabindranath Tagore visits Weimar (May).

Theodor Däubler publishes the final version of his poem *Das Nordlicht*.

1922

The right-wing murder of Foreign Minister Walther Rathenau (June), following the Treaty of Rapallo with the Soviet Union.

Avant-garde *Internationalen Kongress für fortschrittlicher Künstler* (International Congress for Progressive Artists) in Düsseldorf in May followed by the *Konstructivisten-Dadaisten Kongress* (Constructivist-Dadaist Congress) in Weimar in September.

Otto Dix moves to Düsseldorf and publishes his *Zircus* (Circus) portfolio. George Grosz visits Moscow but returns disenchanted by the USSR.

Publication of Hans Prinzhorn's *Bildnerei der Geisteskranken* (Artistry of the Mentally Ill) and of Paul Westheim's survey of post-expressionist trends ('Ein neuer Naturalismus? Eine Rundfrage des Kunstblatts') in *Das Kunstblatt*.

1923

When Germany fails to pay its reparation bill, French and Belgian armies occupy the Ruhr, giving rise to strike action (January). Hyperinflation and mass unemployment. A Communist rising in Hamburg (22–23 October) and a National Socialist putsch in Munich (11 November) fail; both parties are banned, and a state of emergency is declared in Bavaria.

First public broadcasts on German radio. *Erste Bauhaus Ausstellung* (First Bauhaus Exhibition) held in Weimar (August–September).

Publication of Rainer Maria Rilke's *Duineser Elegien* (Duino Elegies) and *Sonette an Orpheus* (Sonnets to Orpheus), and Stefan Zweig's *Amok*.

1924

German unemployment reaches 2.6 million, with inflation at unprecedented levels; elections to the Reichstag see gains for Social Democrats.

The Dawes Plan adjusts German reparations and proposes an end to French occupation of the Ruhr.

Otto Dix publishes his *Der Krieg* (The War) portfolio; there is public controversy around the purchase of his *Schutzengraben* (The Trench) 1920–3 by the Wallraf-Richartz-Museum, Cologne (the work was later destroyed by the Nazis).

Alexander Kanoldt works in Italy.

Publication of Thomas Mann's *Der Zauberberg* (The Magic Mountain), and Joseph Roth's *Die Rebellion* (Rebellion).

1925

French troops withdraw from the Ruhr. Paul von Hindenburg is elected German President and allows Adolf Hitler to re-form the National Socialist party.

Gustav Friedrich Hartlaub organises the *Neue Sachlichkeit: Deutsche Malerei seit dem Expressionismus* (New Objectivity: German Art since Expressionism) exhibition at the Kunsthalle

Mannheim (14 June–13 September); it travels to Dresden (18 October–22 November) and Chemnitz (12 December–17 January 1926).

Franz Roh's *Nach-Expressionismus: Magischer Realismus. Probleme der neuesten europäischen Malerei* (Post-expressionism: Magic Realism. Problems of the New European Painting) is published in December.

Christian Schad moves from Naples to Vienna. Otto Dix moves to Berlin.

Alban Berg's opera *Wozzeck* is produced in Berlin.

1926

Germany joins League of Nations.

Alexander Kanoldt is appointed as professor at the Breslau Academy (in present-day Wrocław, Poland).

The *Neue Sachlichkeit* exhibition continues in a modified form to Erfurt (31 January–28 February), Dessau (from 7 March), Halle (from 18 April) and Jena (16 May–13 June).

The new Bauhaus building, designed by Walter Gropius, is inaugurated at Dessau (December).

Otto Dix's first solo show (Galerie Nierendorf, Berlin, and Galerie Thannhauser, Munich).

1927

Max Beckmann is awarded the Reichsehrenpreis Deutsche Kunst (Honorary Empire Prize of German Art). August Sander presents *Menschen des 20. Jahrhunderts* (People of the 20th Century) at the Kunstverein, Cologne (November). Otto Dix is appointed a professor at the Dresden Academy; Franz Radziwill studies under him.

Christian Schad relocates to Berlin.

Film releases of Walter Ruttmann's *Berlin: Die Sinfonie der Großstadt* (Berlin – Symphony of a Great City), Fritz Lang's *Metropolis*, and Sergei Eisenstein's *Battleship Potemkin*.

1928

The Social Democrats dominate the Reichstag election with 153 seats; the Communists hold 54 seats, and the National Socialists 12.

Hannes Meyer becomes the new director of the Bauhaus (April). The *Internationalen Presse-Ausstellung* (International Press Exhibition) is held at the Staatshaus, Cologne (August). Erich Maria Remarque publishes the anti-war book *Im Westen nichts Neues* (All Quiet on the Western Front).

Bertolt Brecht and Kurt Weill collaborate on *Die Dreigroschenoper* (The Threepenny Opera).

Albert Renger-Patzsch publishes his photographs in *Die Welt ist shön* (The World is Beautiful).

Nazi theorist Paul Schultze-Naumburg publishes the racist *Kunst und Rasse* (Art and Race).

1929

24 October: The Wall Street Crash sets off a worldwide economic crisis.

Alfred Döblin publishes *Berlin Alexanderplatz* and an introduction to August Sander's photographic book *Antlitz der Zeit* (Face of the Times).

The *Internationale Ausstellung des Deutschen Werkbunds Film und Foto* (Deutschen Werkbunds International Exhibition of Film and Photo) is held in the Städtische Ausstellungshallen, Stuttgart (May–July).

First performance of Paul Hindemith's opera *Neues vom Tage* (News of the Day).

Release of Georg Wilhelm Pabst's film *Die Büchse der Pandora* (Pandora's Box) starring Louise Brooks.

1930

September: Reparations re-negotiated under the Young Plan. The Socialists are the largest party in the Reichstag elections but the National Socialists increase from 12 to 107 seats.

Max Beckmann shows at the Venice Biennale. Release of Josef von Sternberg's *Der blaue Engel* (The Blue Angel) starring Marlene Dietrich.

Robert Musil publishes the first volume of *Der Mann ohne Eigenschaften* (The Man without Qualities).

Bertolt Brecht and Kurt Weill collaborate on *Aufstieg und Fall der Stadt Mahagonny* (Rise and Fall of the City of Mahagonny).

1931

Economic crisis across Europe.
In Germany there are 5.7 million unemployed.

Irmgard Keun publishes *Gilgi, eine von uns* (Gilgi, One of Us).

Herbert Gurschner's *Verkündigung* (The Annunciation) 1929–30 is given to the Tate Gallery, London.

1932

Paul von Hindenburg is re-elected as German President. The National Socialists win the July general election without an overall majority.

Otto Dix's *War* triptych (1932) is shown at the Prussian Academy of Arts. A film version of Irmgard Keun's *Gilgi, eine von uns* is released; her second novel, *Das Kunstseidene Mädchen* (The Artificial Silk Girl), is published.

Right-wing officials close the Bauhaus in Dessau, the Academy of Art in Breslau and dismiss teaching staff at the Folkwang school of Design in Essen. Paul Schultze-Naumburg's *Kampf um die Kunst* (Struggle for Art) sets out the significance of art for the National Socialists.

1933

30 January: Adolf Hitler becomes the Chancellor of Germany. The Reichstag fire (27 February) is blamed on the Communists and leads to the outlawing of the Communist and Socialist parties and the dissolution of the trade unions. Dachau concentration camp is established. The Enabling Act (March) creates dictatorial power for Hitler.

March: Culture is placed under Joseph Goebbels's Ministry of Propaganda. The campaign against 'degenerate' modernist art gathers momentum. Gustav Friedrich Hartlaub is among the museum directors dismissed, along with artists and academics across Germany. Many intellectuals go into exile.

George Grosz leaves for the USA. Heinrich Maria Davringhausen moves to France. Otto Dix moves to Lake Constance.

1934

President Paul von Hindenburg dies (August); Hitler assumes the title of Führer.

August: Andrei Zhdanov establishes socialist realism as the official literary style in the USSR.

Otto Dix paints *Triumph des Todes* (Triumph of Death).

1935

September: Racial laws strip German Jews of citizenship.

1936

March: Re-occupation of the demilitarised Rhineland.

July: Outbreak of the Spanish Civil War.

August: Olympic Games in Berlin.

November: Joseph Goebbels bans art criticism in favour of description.

Irmgard Keun emigrates to the Netherlands

1937

26 April: In support of Nationalist forces in the Spanish Civil War, the German Condor Legion bombs the Basque town of Guernica.

The *Grosse Deutsche Kunstausstellung* (Great German Art Exhibition) of official realist art and the contrasting *Entartete Kunst* (Degenerate Art Exhibition) both open in Munich; the latter (with a catalogue featuring a sculpture by Otto Freundlich on the cover) attracts more than two million visitors. Max Beckmann moves to Amsterdam after more than 500 of his works are confiscated from German public collections.

1938

11–14 March: Anschluss: the German annexation of Austria.

29 September: The Munich Agreement allows German annexation of Sudetenland in Czechoslovakia.

9–10 November: Kristallnacht: the Nazis' coordinated assault on Jews.

July: *Twentieth Century German Art*, New Burlington Galleries, London, is a repost to the Degenerate Art show of the previous year. Max Beckmann delivers 'On My Painting'.

1939

15 March: The German invasion of Czechoslovakia.

1 September: The German invasion of Poland triggers a declaration of war by the British and French.

NOTES

INTRODUCTION:
'THE INTERIOR FIGURE OF
THE EXTERIOR WORLD'

1 Walter Benjamin, 'The Storyteller: Reflections on the Works of Nikolai Leskov' (in *Orient und Okzident* 1936, *Schrifften*, Frankfurt-am-Main 1955), trans. Harry Zohn in Hannah Arendt (ed.), *Illuminations*, New York and London 1968, 1973, p.84.

2 Both Klee and Campendonk were associated with *Der Blaue Reiter*, the expressionist grouping in Munich, and Klee had a breakthrough postwar exhibition at the Galerie Neue Kunst Hans Goltz there in the summer of 1920; see Matthew Gale (ed.), *The EY Exhibition: Paul Klee; Making Visible*, exh. cat., Tate Modern, London 2013, pp.46–9. Although based in Paris and Vitebsk, Chagall had influential exhibitions at the bastion of expressionism, Herwarth Walden's Galerie Der Sturm in Berlin in 1914 and 1917.

3 The image may evoke the words of the Lord at the beginning of *Faust*: 'Though now his service be as a tangled skein | Yet will I lead him soon to perfect vision. | The gardener knows, when the young tree is green, | 'Twill glad the years with blossom and fruition.' (Johann Wolfgang von Goethe, *Faust Parts I and II*, trans. Albert G. Latham, London 1908, p.22.)

4 See Jean Cocteau's *Rappel à l'ordre*, Paris 1926.

5 Paul Westheim, 'Notizien', *Das Kunstblatt*, no.3, October 1919, cited in Stephanie Barron, 'New Objectivity: German Realism after Expressionism', in Stephanie Barron (ed.), *New Objectivity: Modern German Art in the Weimar Republic 1919–33*, exh. cat., Los Angeles County Museum of Art, 2015, p.16.

6 Klee and Ernst encountered *Valori plastici* in the Galerie Neue Kunst Hans Goltz in Munich, see William A. Camfield, *Max Ernst: Dada and the Dawn of Surrealism*, exh. cat., Museum of Modern Art, New York 1993, p.57.

7 The survival of a copy of the international (French language) edition of *Valori plastici* (no.3, 1920) stamped with Roh's name and Munich address attests to his interest.

8 In *Der Cicerone*, no.9, 1920.

9 *Berliner Tageblatt*, 7 April 1921, extracted and translated in a *Valori plastici* flier, reproduced in Maurizio Fagiolo dell'Arco, *Giorgio de Chirico: Il tempo di Valori plastici 1918–1922*, Rome 1982, p.62.

10 Gustav Friedrich Hartlaub in Paul Westheim, 'Ein Neue Naturalismus? Eine Rundfrage des Kunstblatts', *Das Kunstblatt*, no.9, 1922, cited in Irene Guenther, 'Magic Realism, New Objectivity, and the Arts during the Weimar Republic', in Lois Parkinson Zamora and Wendy B. Faris (eds), *Magical Realism: Theory, History, Community*, Durham, NC, and London 1995, p.41.

11 Christian Fuhrmeister, 'Hartlaub and Roh: Cooperation and Competition in Popularizing New Objectivity', in Barron 2015, p.43.

12 See Leah Dickerman, 'Bauhaus Fundamentals', in Barry Bergdoll and Leah Dickerman (eds), *Bauhaus 1919–1933: Workshops for Modernity*, exh. cat., Museum of Modern Art, New York 2009, pp.23, 204.

13 Fuhrmeister (Barron 2015, p.47 n.1) gives the known dates as: Mannheim, 14 June–13 September 1925; Dresden, 18 October–22 November; Chemnitz, 12 December–17 January 1926; Erfurt, 31 January–28 February; Dessau, from 7 March; Halle, from 18 April; Jena, 16 May–13 June 1926. Klee noted Harlaub's Dessau lecture on 29 March 1926, see Paul Klee, *Lettres de l'époque du Bauhaus (1920–1930)*, trans. Anne-Sophie Petit-Emptaz, Tours 2004, p.111.

14 G.F. Hartlaub, 'Zum Geleit', in *Neue Sachlichkeit: Deutsche Malerei seit dem Expressionismus*, exh. cat., Städtische Kunsthalle, Mannheim 1925, trans. Nancy Roth in Rose-Carol Washton Long (ed.), *German Expressionism: Documents from the End of the Wilhelmine Empire to the Rise of National Socialism*, New York 1993, p.291.

15 Noted at the time of an exhibition of the Communist affiliated *Die Rote Gruppe* in Berlin in 1924; see Martin Ignatius Gaughan, *German Art 1907–1937: Modernism and Modernisations*, Oxford and Bern 2007, pp.172–3. Uwe M. Scheede, writing in the 1970s, notes that this distinction persisted in both East and West Germany ('Vérisme et nouvelle objectivité', in Werner Spies and Jean-Hubert Martin (eds), *Paris-Berlin 1900–1933: Rapports et contrastes franco-allemagne*, exh. cat., Centre Georges Pompidou, Paris 1978, p.184).

16 *Nach-Expressionismus: Magischer Realismus. Probleme der neuesten europäschen Malerei*, Leipzig 1925. For this text and its relation to the later adoption of the term in Latin America, see Guenther 1995, pp.33–73.

17 Fuhrmeister (Barron 2015, p.46) notes that the publisher told Roh on 10 December 1925 that the wrapper read '*Die Kunst des neuen Sachlichkeit*' (The Art of the New Objectivity).

18 Hartlaub's concentration on German art may reflect the limitations of sourcing works locally over the openness of writing a book.

19 Sigmund Freud, 'Das Unheimliche', *Imago*, vol.5, nos 5-6, 1919, pp.297–324, trans. Alix Strachey in James Strachey (ed.), *The Standard Edition of the Complete Psychological Works of Sigmund Freud, vol.17, An Infantile Neurosis and Other Works*, London 1975, pp.219–52.

20 Franz Roh, 'Magical Realism: Post-Expressionism', in Zamora and Faris 1995, pp.23–4.

21 Ibid., pp.29–30.

22 Franz Roh, 'Post-Expressionist Schema', trans. Edward Dimendberg in Anton Kaes, Martin Jay and Edward Dimendberg (eds), *The Weimar Republic Sourcebook*, Berkeley, Los Angeles and London 1994, p.493.

23 See Fuhrmeister's careful analysis, in Barron 2015, pp.40–8.

24 See Andrew Hemingway, 'Franz Roh's *Nach-Expressionismus* and the *Weltanschauung* of the Weimar Republic', *German Studies Review*, vol.40, no.2, 2017, pp.267–88.

25 Wieland Schmied, 'Neue Sachlichkeit and German Realism of the Twenties', in *Neue Sachlichkeit and German Realism of the Twenties*, exh. cat., Hayward Gallery, London 1978, p.32.

THE CIRCUS: 'ABNORMAL SITUATIONS'

1 Otto Dix, quoted in Mathias Eberle, *World War I and the Weimar Artists*, New Haven and London 1985, p.42.

2 Other identified works in this series include *Der Akrobat* 1921, shown in *Realismus der Zwanziger Jahre*, exh. cat., Galerie Michael Hasenclever, Munich 1980, fig.12; and *Akrobat Schulz* 1924, in *Anti:modern: Salzburg in the Heart of Europe between Tradition and Renewal*, exh. cat., Museum der Moderne Salzburg, 2016.

3 Christian Rogowski, 'Introduction: Images and Imaginaries', in Rogowski (ed.), *The Many Faces of Weimar Cinema: Rediscovering Germany's Filmic Legacy*, New York 2010, p.4.

4 Hans Fallada, *Bauern, Bonzen und Bomben*, Berlin 1931, translated by Michael Hofmann as *A Small Circus*, London 2013.

5 Christiane Zeiller, 'Max Beckmann's Passion for the Circus, as Reflected in his Sketchbooks', in Sebastian Karnatz, *Max Beckmann: The World as a Stage*, exh. cat., Kunsthalle Bremen 2017, p.64.

6 *Der Querschnitt*, vol. 6, no. 12, issue 12, 1926, p.967.

7 For an extended account of this via the August Sander photograph *Circus Artistes* 1926–32 (p.31), see Katherine Tubb, 'Face to Face? An Ethical Encounter with Germany's Dark Strangers in August Sander's *People of the Twentieth Century*', *Tate Papers*, no.19, Spring 2013, http://www.tate.org.uk/research/publications/tate-papers/19/face-to-face-an-ethical-encounter-with-germany-dark-strangers-in-august-sanders-people-of-the-twentieth-century, accessed 4 December 2017.

8 A research project titled 'Diverging Fates' is currently underway, coordinated by the centre for Nordic Studies at the University of Helsinki (2017–18). Its objective is to examine 'the histories and divergent fates of circus owners, circus families and performers in Europe under National Socialism'. It cites oral histories as one of the main strategies for documenting the lives of those who travelled with circus troupes in the era of National Socialism: http://www.divergingfates.eu/index.php/2017/02/22/project-description/

9 See Michael White, 'The Grosz Case: Paranoia, Self hatred and Anti-Semitism', *Oxford Art Journal*, vol.30, no.3, 2007, pp.431–53.

10 Kristin Makholm, 'Prints in Germany 1905–1923', *Bulletin (Saint Louis Art Museum)*, New Series, vol.20, no.4, Summer 1993, p.24.

11 Beth Irwin Lewis, 'Lustmord: Inside the Windows of the Metropolis,' in Katharina von Ankum (ed.), *Women in the Metropolis: Gender and Modernity in Weimar Culture*, Berkeley and Los Angeles 1997, p. 226.

12 George Grosz, *Gedichte und Gesänge*, 1916–17, Litomyšl 1932, translated in Katharina von Ankum (ed.), ibid., p.204.

13 White 2007, pp.431–53.

14 Theodor Däubler, 'Georg [sic] Grosz,' *Die Weissen Blätter* 3, October–December 1916, pp.167–70; and 'George Grosz', *Das Kunstblatt*, I March 1917, pp.80–2, quoted in Lewis 1997, p.204.

15 Lewis 1997, p.220.

16 Quoted in Eva Karcher, *Otto Dix, 1891–1969: Leben und Werk*, Cologne 1988, p.43.

FROM THE STREET TO THE STUDIO: 'PLEASURABLE ABUNDANCE'

1 Werner Gräff, 'Pleasurable Abundance – by Means of New Technology', in Detlef Mertins and Michael W. Jennings (eds), *G: An Avant-Garde Journal of Art, Architecture, Design, and Film, 1923–1926*, trans. Steven Lindberg with Margareta Ingrid Christian, Los Angeles 2010, London 2011, p.190; originally published in *G*, no.4, March 1926, p.190.

2 Stefan Zweig, 'Die Monotonisierung der Welt', *Berliner Börsen-Courier*, February 1925, trans. Don Reneau in Anton Kaes, Martin Jay and Edward Dimendberg (eds), *The Weimar Republic Sourcebook*, Berkeley, Los Angeles and London 1994, pp.397–400. See also Martin Ignatius Gaughan, *German Art 1907–1937: Modernism and Modernisation (German Linguistic and Cultural Studies, vol.19)*, Oxford and Bern 2007, p.177.

3 Gräff 1926.

4 Eric D. Weitz, *Weimar Germany: Promise and Tragedy*, Princeton 2007, p.41, cited in Jacqueline Strecker, 'Introduction', *The Mad Square: Modernity in German Art 1910–37*, exh. cat., Art Gallery of New South Wales, Sydney 2011, p.24.

5 See Hans M. Wingler, *Bauhaus*, trans. Wolfgang Jabs and Basil Gilbert, Cambridge, MA 1993.

6 *Erste Bauhausausstellung*, Staatliche Bauhaus, Weimar, August–September 1923, *Internationalen Presse-Ausstellung*, Staatshaus, Cologne, from August 1928, and *Internationale Ausstellung des Deutschen Werkbunds Film und Foto*, Städtische Ausstellungshallen Stuttgart, May–July 1929.

7 Siegfried Kracauer, 'Die Angestellten', *Frankfurter Zeitung*, 1929 and Frankfurt 1971, quoted in Gaughan 2007, p.245. See also ibid., pp.225–52.

8 'George Grosz', *G*, no.3, June 1924, p.153, translated in Mertins and Jennings 2011, p.153.

9 See David King and Ernst Volland, *John Heartfield: Laughter is a Devastating Weapon*, London 2015.

10 Seen, for instance, in Hans Windisch, *Das Lichtbild Jahresschau*, Berlin 1927.

11 Franz Roh and Jan Tschichold, *Foto-Auge*, Stuttgart 1929.

12 Siegfried Kracauer, 'Die Photographie', *Frankfurter Zeitung*, 28 October 1927, quoted in Ute Eskildsen, 'Photography and the Neue Sachlichkeit movement', in *Neue Sachlichkeit and German Realism of the Twenties*, exh. cat., Hayward Gallery, London 1979, p.91. See also Gaughan 2007, pp.217–24.

13 See Steve Plumb, *Neue Sachlichkeit 1918–33: Unity and Diversity of an Art Movement*, Amsterdam and New York 2006, pp.97–104.

14 See Maria Makela, 'New Women, New Man, New Objectivity', in Stephanie Barron (ed.), *New Objectivity: Modern German Art in the Weimar Republic 1919–33*, exh. cat., Los Angeles County Museum of Art, 2015, pp.51–63.

[15] Rudolf Schlichter, *Zwischenwelt: Ein Intermezzo*, Berlin 1931 and *Das widerspenstige Fleisch*, Berlin 1932, cited in Michael White, *Generation Dada: The Berlin Avant-Garde and the First World War*, New Haven and London 2013, pp.25, 319, n.38.

[16] See Marsha Meskimmon, *We Weren't Modern Enough: Women Artists and the Limits of German Modernism*, London 1999.

[17] Herbert Read, *Art Now: An Introduction to the Theory of Modern Painting and Sculpture*, London 1933, pp.92–3.

THE CABARET: 'LOOKING FOR ADVENTURE'

[1] Curt Moreck (pseudonym of Konrad Haemmerling), 'We Will Show You Berlin', first published as 'Wir zeigen Ihnen Berlin', in *Führer durch das "lasterhafte" Berlin*, Leipzig 1930, in Anton Kaes, Martin Jay and Edward Dimendberg (eds), *The Weimar Republic Sourcebook*, Berkeley, Los Angeles and London 1994, p.562. A more recent publication gives the English translation, 'A Guide to "Licentious" Berlin', trans. Iain Boyd Whyte, in Boyd Whyte and David Frisby (eds) *Metropolis Berlin: 1880–1940*, Berkeley 2012, p.540.

[2] Alan Lareau, 'The Blonde Lady Sings: Women in Weimar Cabaret', in Christiane Schönfeld (ed.), *Practicing Modernity: Female Creativity in the Weimar Republic*, Würzburg 2006, p.192.

[3] Presented in Rose Lee Goldberg, 'Performance – Art for All?', *Art Journal*, vol.40, no.1/2: Modernism, Revisionism, Plurism, and Post-Modernism, Autumn–Winter 1980, pp.369–76.

[4] Robert McAlmon and Kay Boyle, *Being Geniuses Together: 1920–1930*, London 1984, p.98.

[5] Alan Lareau, 'The German Cabaret Movement during the Weimar Republic', *Theatre Journal*, vol.43, no.4, December 1991, p.474.

[6] Jill Lloyd, 'Urban Exoticism in the Cabaret and Circus', in J. Lloyd, *German Expressionism: Primitivism and Modernity*, New Haven 1991, pp.85–101.

[7] Karl Eric Toepfer, *Empire of Ecstasy: Nudity and Movement in Germany Body Culture 1910–1935*, Berkeley 1997, p.238.

[8] Plate LI: H.B. Goodwin, 'Primavera and Beatrice Mariagraete', in F.J. Mortimer (ed.), *Photograms of the Year 1916: The Annual Review of the World's Pictorial Photographic Work*, London 1916.

[9] There are relatively few dedicated publications on Mammen, perhaps owing to the brevity in output of her best-known works in the Weimar era. Nonetheless, the following publications have been especially enlightening: Annelie Lütgens, 'The Conspiracy of Women: Images of City Life in the Work of Jeanne Mammen', in Katharina von Ankum (ed.), *Women in the Metropolis: Gender and Modernity in Weimar Culture*, Los Angeles 1997; Annelie Lütgens, 'Jeanne Mammen', in Louise R. Noun (ed.), *Three Women Artists of the Weimar Era: Hannah Höch, Käthe Kollwitz, Jeanne Mammen*, exh. cat., Des Moines Art Center, IA 1994, pp.92–102; and Katharina Sykora, 'Jeanne Mammen', *Woman's Art Journal*, vol.9, no.2, Autumn 1988–Winter 1989, pp.28–31.

[10] Lütgens 1994, p.94; Walter Benjamin, *The Arcades Project*, Rolf Tiedemann (ed.), trans. Howard Eiland and Kevin McLaughlin, New York 2002.

FAITH AND MAGIC: 'A HIGHER DEGREE OF REALITY'

[1] Extracted and translated as Franz Roh, 'Post-Expressionist Schema', in Anton Kaes, Martin Jay and Edward Dimendberg (eds), *The Weimar Republic Sourcebook*, Berkeley, Los Angeles and London 1994, p.493.

[2] Ann Steiglitz, 'The Reproduction of Agony: toward a Reception-History of Grünewald's *Isenheim Altar* after the First World War', *The Oxford Art Journal*, vol.12, no.2, 1989, p.92.

[3] Wilhelm Hausenstein, *Der Isenheim Altar*, Munich 1919, quoted and translated in Steiglitz 1989, p.93. For other aspects of his writing, see Annie Bourneuf, 'An Art of Privacy? Wilhelm Hausenstein on Paul Klee', in Matthew Gale (ed.), *The EY Exhibition; Paul Klee: Making Visible*, exh. cat., Tate Modern, London 2013, pp.36–42.

[4] See Steiglitz 1989, p.97, who notes the report in *Munchner Neueste Nachrichten*, 28 September 1919. See also Philip McCoust, 'The Isenheim Altarpiece, Part 2: Nationalism, Nazism and Degeneracy', *Journal of Art in Society*, 2014, http://www.artinsociety.com/the-isenheim-altarpiece-pt-2-nationalism-nazism-and-degeneracy.html, accessed 1 September 2017.

[5] Steiglitz 1989, p.93.

[6] Frank Whitford ('The Revolutionary Reactionary', in *Otto Dix 1891–1969*, exh. cat. Tate Gallery, London 1992, p.13) cites a letter from Grosz to Herbert and Amrei Fiedler, 12 October 1934 (in Herbert Knust ed., *George Grosz Briefe 1913–1959*, Reinbeck bei Hamburg 1979, p.202).

[7] See Richard Cork, *A Bitter Truth: Avant-Garde Art and the Great War*, exh. cat., Barbican Art Gallery, London 1994, pp.273–4, 293, 302–6; David Midgley, 'The Ecstacy of Battle: Some German Perspectives on Warfare Between Modernism and Reaction', in Jana Howlett and Rod Mengham (eds), *The Violent Muse: Violence and the Artistic Imagination in Europe, 1910–1939*, Manchester and New York 1994, pp.113–16; and Michael White, *Generation Dada: The Berlin Avant-Garde and the First World War*, New Haven and London 2013, p.352, n.37.

[8] J.B. Manson, 'Foreword', *Paintings, Watercolours and Wodcuts by Herbert Gurschner (Tyrolese Artist)*, exh. cat., Fine Arts Society, London 1931, p.5.

[9] See the discussion of Roh in this respect in Andrew Hemingway, 'Franz Roh's *nach-Expressionismus* and the *Weltanschauung* of the Weimar Republic', *German Studies Review*, vol.40, no.2, 2017, pp.274–5.

[10] See Kris Manjapra, 'The Anticolonial Laboratory: Indian Nationalist Diaspora in German-Speaking Europe', in Regina Bittner and Kathrin Rhomberg (eds), *The Bauhaus in Calcutta: An Encounter of the Cosmopolitan Avant-Garde*, Ostfildern 2013, pp.151–61.

[11] See, for instance, *Itten / Klee: Kosmos / Farbe*, exh. cat., Kunstmuseum, Bern 2012.

[12] See also the rather more restrained visionary sky in Otto Dix's *Portrait of the Poet Theodor Däubler* 1927, Museum Ludwig, Cologne.

[13] *Das Nordlicht*, Florence 1910, Leipzig 1921, http://gutenberg.spiegel.de/buch/das-nordlicht-erster-teil-das-mittelmeer-genfer-ausgabe-8086/2, accessed 7 August 2017. See also Sergio Lambiase, 'Theodor Däubler', in Lea Vergine (ed.), *Capri 1905–1940*, Milan 2003

[14] Rainer Maria Rilke, *Duino Elegies*, trans. and introduced by J.B. Leishman and Stephen Spender, revised, London 1948.

[15] 'The Tenth Elegy', ibid., p.91.

[16] 'Appendix IV: The Task of Transformation', ibid., p.159, quoting Rilke to Witold von Hulewicz (his Polish translator), 13 November 1925.

[17] See White 2013, pp.12–13, 259.

[18] Hartlaub to Alfred H. Barr Jr, on 8 July 1929, in Alfred H. Barr Jr, *German Painting and Sculpture (1905–1930)*, exh. cat., Museum of Modern Art, New York 1931, p.13.

[19] Misch Orend, 'Der magische Realismus', *Klingsor, Siebenbürische Zeitschrift*, January 1928, p.25, translated as 'Magical Realism', in Kaes, Jay and Dimendberg 1994, p.494.

[20] George Grosz, 'Unter anderem ein Wort für die deutsche Tradition', *Das Kunstblatt*, vol.15, no.3, 1931, pp.79–84, translated as 'Among Other Things, a Word for German Tradition', in Kaes, Jay and Dimendberg 1994, p.501.

[21] 'Theses on the Philosophy of History', Spring 1940, *Neue Rundschau*, vol.61, no.3, 1950, in Walter Benjamin, *Illuminations*, Hannah Arendt (ed.), trans. Harry Zohn, London 1970, pp.259–60.

[22] Thomas Mann, *Doktor Faustus: Das Leben des deutschen Tonsetzers Adrian Leverkühn, erzählt von einem Freundei*, Berlin 1947 trans. H.T. Lowe-Porter as *Doctor Faustus: The Life of the German Composer Adrian Leverkühn, As Told by a Friend*, London 1949 and Harmondsworth 1968.

CODA: 'FROM THE VISIBLE TO THE INVISIBLE''

[1] Marko Daniel, 'Chronology', in *Art and Power: Europe Under the Dictators 1930–45*, exh. cat., Hayward Gallery, London 1995, p.21; Gertje R. Utley, *Picasso: The Communist Years*, New Haven and London 2000, p.136.

[2] Quoted in Herbert Read, *Art and Society*, London 1936, 1956, p.129.

[3] Ibid., pp.129–33.

[4] Herbert Read, *Surrealism*, London 1936, p.89.

[5] Adolf Hitler, 'Peroration of Speech at the Great German Art Exhibition 1937', trans. by John Willett, in *Art and Power: Europe Under the Dictators 1930–45*, exh. cat., Hayward Gallery, London 1995, p.338.

[6] Max Beckmann, *On My Painting*, Foreword by Mayen Beckmann, Afterword by Sean Rainbird, London 2003, p.17.

[7] Simon J. Dell, 'Festival and Revolution: the Popular Front in France and the Press Coverage of the Strikes of 1936', *Art History*, vol.23, no.4, November 2000, pp.599–621; see also Sarah Wilson, *Picasso/Marx and Socialist Realism in France*, Liverpool 2013.

[8] Aragon in 'Painting and Reality: A Discussion', *transition: A Quarterly Review*, no.25, Fall 1936, p.122.

[9] Le Corbusier, 'The Quarrel with Realism: The Destiny of Painting', in J.L. Martin, Ben Nicholson and Naum Gabo (eds), *Circle: International Survey of Constructive Art*, London 1937, 1971, p.74.

[10] Beckmann 2003, p.11.

EXHIBITED WORKS

GEC = The George Economou Collection

Max Beckmann (1884–1950)
Frau Ullstein (Portrait of a Woman)
Frau Ullstein (Porträt einer Frau) 1920
Graphite on paper, 33 × 23.8
GEC 19200037, p.25

Anni (Girl with Fan)
Anni (Mädchen mit Fächer) 1942
Oil paint on canvas, 84.6 × 44.5
GEC 19420007, p.77

Richard Biringer (1877–1947)
Krupp Works, Engers am Rhein
Krupp-Werke, Engers am Rhein 1925
Oil paint on canvas, 67.5 × 49.5
GEC 19250013, p.46

Albert Birkle (1900–1986)
The Acrobat Schulz V
Der Akrobat Schulz V 1921
Tempera and chalk on paper mounted
on cardboard, 70.4 × 50
GEC 19210008, p.23

Crucifixion
Kreuzigung 1921
Oil paint on board, 92 × 60.7
GEC 19210029, p.87 (detail, p.82)

The Hermit
Die Eremit 1921
Oil paint on canvas, 91 × 60.5
GEC 19210028, p.86

Passau 1925
Oil paint on hardboard, 51 × 71
GEC 020153, p.47

Heinrich Campendonk (1889–1957)
The Rider II
Der Reiter II 1919
Watercolour on paper mounted
on cardboard, 35.3 × 39.3
GEC 19190009, p.9

Marc Chagall (1887–1985)
The Green Donkey
L'Ane vert 1911
Gouache on board, 32.4 × 41.3
Tate, Presented by Lady Clerk 1947
[N05758], p.9

Lovis Corinth (1858–1925)
Magdalen with Pearls in her Hair
Magdalena mit Perlenkette im Haar 1919
Oil paint on canvas, 71.5 × 47.6
Tate, Purchased 1991 [T05866], p.88

Heinrich Maria Davringhausen (1894–1970)
The Poet Däubler
Der Dichter Däubler 1917
Oil paint on canvas, 181 × 160.3
GEC 19170005, p.11 (detail, p.6)

Prosper de Troyer (1880–1961)
Erik Satie (The Prelude)
Erik Satie (Le prélude) 1925
Oil paint on canvas, 210 × 145
GEC 19250021, p.75

Heinrich Harry Deierling (1894–1989)
The Gardener
Der Gärtner 1920
Oil paint on canvas, 187 × 119.5
GEC 19200007, p.12

Rudolf Dischinger (1904–1988)
Backyard Balcony
Hinterhaus-Balkon 1935
Oil paint on canvas, 58 × 50
GEC 19350004, p.50

Otto Dix (1891–1969)
Portrait of Bruno Alexander Roscher
Bildnis Bruno Alexander Roscher 1915
Oil paint on board, 67 × 50.5
GEC 19150001, p.13

Butcher Shop
Fleischerladen 1920
Etching, drypoint on paper, 49.5 × 33.8
plate 29.5 × 25.8
GEC 036, p.32

Billiard Players
Billiardspieler 1920
Etching, drypoint on paper, 34 × 48.8
plate 22.5 × 33.3
GEC 047, p.32

Sailor and Girl
Matrose und Mädchen 1920
Etching, drypoint on paper, 48.7 × 34.2
plate 30 × 24.8
GEC 049, p.32

Lust Murderer
Lustmörder 1920
Etching on paper, 49 × 34.1
plate 30 × 25.7
GEC 051, p.35

Zirkus
Circus 1922 (print portfolio)

The Scorners of Death
Die Verächter des Todes 1922
Etching, drypoint on paper,
49.7 × 42.8, plate 34.7 × 27.7
GEC 067, p.26

Illusion Act
Illusionsakt 1922
Etching, drypoint on paper
49.5 × 42.9, plate 30 × 25.7
GEC 069, p.27

Sketch 1922
Etching, drypoint on paper,
49.7 × 42.9, plate 39.4 × 29.7
GEC 070, p.27

Balancing Act
Balanceakt 1922
Etching, drypoint on paper,
49.6 × 42.9, plate 29.9 × 19.7
GEC 071, p.27

Maud Arizona
(Suleika, The Tattooed Wonder)
Maud Arizona
(Suleika, das tätowierte Wunder) 1922
Etching, drypoint on paper,
49.8 × 42.8, plate 29.9 × 19.8
GEC 072, p.27

International Riding Act
Internationaler Reitakt 1922
Etching, drypoint on paper,
49.6 × 43.1
plate 39.9 × 29.8
GEC 074, p.28

American Riding Act
Amerikanischer Reitakt 1922
Etching, drypoint on paper,
49.7 × 42.9
plate 34.7 × 30.9
GEC 075, p.28

Technical Personnel
Technisches Personal 1922
Etching, drypoint on paper,
49.7 × 42.6
plate 30 × 19.8
GEC 076, p.28

Lili, The Queen of the Air
Lili, die Königin der Luft 1922
Etching, drypoint on paper,
49.7 × 42.8
plate 29.9 × 19.8
GEC 077, p.28

Tamer
Dompteuse 1922
Etching, drypoint on paper,
49.6 × 42.9, plate 39.9 × 29.7
GEC 078, p.29

Performers
Artisten 1922
Etching, drypoint on paper, 49.2 × 34
plate 29.9 × 25.8
GEC 079, p.32

Lust Murder
Lustmord 1922
Watercolour, ink and graphite on paper,
48.5 × 36.5
GEC 19220016, p.35

Circus Scene (Riding Act)
Zirkusszene (Reitakt) 1923
Watercolour, pen and ink on paper,
38.1 × 27.6
GEC 19230022, p.33 (detail, p.20)

Josef Eberz (1880–1942)
Dancer (Beatrice Mariagraete)
Tänzerin (Beatrice Mariagraete) 1923
Oil paint on canvas, 158 × 78.5
GEC 19230005, p.73

Conrad Felixmüller (1897–1977)
Portrait of Ernst Buchholz
Bildnis Ernst Buchholz 1921
Oil paint on canvas, 90 × 75
GEC 19210030, p.51

The Beggar of Prachatice
Der Bettler von Prachatitz 1924
Watercolour, gouache and graphite
on paper, 50 × 64.5
GEC 19240057, p.52

Otto Griebel (1895–1972)
Two Women
Zwei Frauen 1924
Watercolour on cardboard, 63.8 × 45
GEC 19240054, p.77

Carl Grossberg (1894–1940)
Rokin Street, Amsterdam
Rokin, Amsterdam 1925
Tempera on panel, 50.5 × 60.3
GEC 19250019, p.53

George Grosz (1893–1959)
Suicide
Selbstmörder 1916
Oil paint on canvas, 100 × 77.5
Tate, Purchased with assistance from the Art Fund 1976 [T02053], p.17

Drawing for 'The Mirror of the Bourgeoisie'
Drawing for 'Der Spiesser-Spiegel' c.1925
Ink on paper, 62.9 × 50.5
Tate, Presented by the Contemporary Art Society 1955 [T00020], p.39

A Married Couple
Ehepaar 1930
Watercolour on paper, 66 × 47.3
Tate, Presented by the Contemporary Art Society 1955 [T00019], p.41

Self-Portrait with Model in the Studio
Selbstbildnis mit Modell im Atelier 1930–7
Watercolour, gouache, pen and ink on paper, 50.5 × 44
GEC 19300020, p.41

Hans Grundig (1901–1958)
Girl with Pink Hat
Mädchen mit rosa Hut 1925
Oil paint on cardboard, 70.4 × 50
GEC 19250022, p.56

Lea Grundig (1906–1977)
Into the Abyss
In den Abgrund 1943
Pen and ink on cardboard, 44 × 56
GEC 19430006, p.95

Herbert Gurschner (1901–1975)
Triumph of Death
Triumph des Todes 1927
Oil paint on canvas, 109 × 89.5
GEC 19270002, p.92

Lazarus (The Workers)
Lazarus (Die Arbeiter) 1928
Oil paint on canvas, 92 × 69
GEC 19280004, p.93

Bean Ingram 1928
Oil paint on canvas, 107 × 67.5
GEC 19280002, p.57

The Annunciation
Verkündigung 1929–30
Oil paint on canvas, 161.7 × 191.1
Tate, Presented by Lord Duveen 1931 [N04593], p.89

Japanese Lady
Japanische Dame 1932
Oil paint on canvas, 87 × 61
GEC 19320003, p.56

August Heitmüller (1873–1935)
Self-Portrait
Selbstbildnis 1926
Oil paint on canvas, 90 × 70.5
GEC 19260011, p.60

Karl Otto Hy (1904–1992)
Anna 1932
Oil paint on canvas, 95 × 67.5
GEC 19320014, p.60

Alexander Kanoldt (1881–1939)
Monastery Chapel of Säben
Kapelle in Südtirol 1920
Oil paint on canvas, 35 × 29
GEC 19200028, p.61

Paul Klee (1879–1940)
They're Biting
Sie beissen an 1920
Watercolour and oil paint on paper 31.1 × 23.5
Tate, Purchased 1946 [N05658], p.40

Comedy
Komödie 1921
Watercolour and oil paint on paper, 30.5 × 45.4
Tate, Purchased 1946 [N05657], p.40

Jeanne Mammen (1890–1976)
At the Shooting Gallery
An der Schießbude 1929
Watercolour and graphite on vellum, 44.5 × 36
GEC 19290016, p.79 (detail, p.70)

Boring Dolls
Langweilige Puppen 1929
Watercolour and graphite on paper mounted on cardboard, 38.4 × 28.6
GEC 19290013, p.79

Brüderstrasse (Free Room)
Brüderstrasse (Zimmer frei) 1930
Watercolour, ink and graphite on vellum, 47.5 × 34.5
GEC 19300027, p.80

Josef Mangold (1884–1937)
Flower Still Life with Playing Card
Blumenstilleben mit Spielkarte undated
Oil paint on panel, 41 × 31.7
GEC 020426, p.62

Carlo Mense (1886–1965)
Self-Portrait
Selbstbildnis 1918
Oil paint on canvas, 45.7 × 34.3
GEC 19180012, p.13

Portrait of Don Domenico
Bildnis Don Domenico 1924
Oil paint on cardboard, 53.6 × 42
GEC 19240051, p.63

Richard Müller (1874–1954)
In the Studio
Im Atelier 1926
Oil paint on canvas, 107 × 75.5
GEC 19260012, p.64

Sergius Pauser (1896–1970)
Self-Portrait with Mask
Selbstbildnis mit Maske 1926
Oil paint on canvas, 60 × 73
GEC 19260009, p.81

Franz Radziwill (1895–1983)
Conversation about a Paragraph
Gespräch über einen Paragraphen 1929
Oil paint on canvas laid on wood, 79.3 × 101
GEC 19290017, p.65

Christian Schad (1894–1982)
Prof. Holzmeister 1926
Charcoal on paper, 54.2 × 40
GEC 19260013, p.40

Josef Scharl (1896–1954)
Conference / The Group
Konferenz / Die Gruppe 1927
Oil paint on canvas, 81 × 64.5
GEC 19270008, p.68

Otto Rudolf Schatz (1900–1961)
Moon Women
Mondfrauen 1930
Oil paint on canvas, 191.5 × 111
GEC 19300006, p.66

Rudolf Schlichter (1890–1955)
The Artist with Two Hanged Women
Der Künstler mit zwei erhängten Frauen 1924
Watercolour and graphite on paper,
45.3 × 34
GEC 19240058, p.36

Lady with Red Scarf (Speedy with the Moon)
Frauenportrait (Speedy) 1933
Oil paint on canvas, 92.5 × 64.5
GEC 19330012, p.67 (detail, p.42)

Werner Schramm (1898–1970)
Portrait of a Lady in front of the Pont des Arts
Damenbildnis vor der Pont des Arts 1930
Oil paint on panel, 81 × 61
GEC 19300030, p.69

Marie-Louise von Motesiczky (1906–1996)
Portrait of a Russian Student
Porträt eines russischen Studenten 1927
Oil paint on canvas, 82.8 × 54.2
Tate, Presented by the Marie-Louise
von Motesiczky Charitable Trust 2017
[T14867], p.68

Nicolai Wassilieff (1901–1977)
Interior
Innere 1923
Oil paint on canvas, 41 × 30
GEC 19230011, p.63

INDEX

Note: italics indicate pages with images.

CREDITS

Page 14: Stefan Zweig, 'Die unsichtbare Sammlung', 1925, in *The Invisible Collection: Tales of Obsession and Desire*, translation © Anthea Bell, published by Pushkin Press, London 2015.

Page 44: Robert Walser, 'Radio', May–June 1926, in *Microscripts*, copyright © Suhrkamp Verlag Zurich and Frankfurt am Main 1985, translation by Susan Bernofsky, reprinted by permission of New Directions Publishing Corp., New York 2010.

Page 55: Irmgard Keun, *Gilgi, eine von uns*, 1931, in *Gilgi, One of Us*, translation by Geoff Wilkes, reprinted courtesy of Melville House Publishing, Brooklyn and London 2013.

Page 59: Alfred Döblin, *Berlin, Alexanderplatz: The Story of Franz Biberkopf*, translation by Eugene Jolas, London 1931, Penguin Books, Harmondsworth 1978.

Page 91: Joseph Roth, *Die Rebellion*, 1924, translation © 1999 by Michael Hofmann, reproduced with permission of Granta Publications.

Images courtesy of The George Economou Collection: 13 (left), 26, 27 (all), 28 (all), 29, 32 (all), 35 (left), 40 (top right), 51, 60 (left), 65, 69, 86.

Images courtesy of The George Economou Collection (photography Studio Vaharidis): 12, 35 (right), 36, 52, 63 (left), 64, 66, 70, 75, 79 (right), 80.

David Lambert and Joe Humphrys, Tate Photography: cover, 6, 11, 13 (right), 20, 23, 25, 33, 41 (right), 42, 46, 47, 50, 53, 56 (both), 57, 60 (right), 61, 62, 63 (right), 67, 68 (right), 73, 77 (both), 79 (left), 81, 82, 87, 92, 93, 95.

All artworks are © the artists unless otherwise stated below. Every effort has been made to trace the copyright holders of the works reproduced. The publisher apologises for any omissions that may have inadvertently been made.

49 © Albert Renger-Patzsch Archiv/Ann und Jürgen Wilde / DACS 2018. 40 © Christian Schad Stiftung Aschaffenburg/VG Bild-Kunst, Bonn and DACS, London 2018. Front cover (detail) and back cover, 9 (top), 13, 20 (detail), 23, 25, 26, 27, 27 (all), 28, 28 (all), 29, 32 (all), 33, 35, 35, 47, 51, 52, 56, 65, 70 (detail) 77, 79, 79, 80, 82 (detail), 86, 87, 95 © DACS 2018. 75 © DACS 2018, Erven de Troyer / Mark and Tess Uytterhoeven. 31 © Die Photographische Sammlung/SK Stiftung Kultur – August Sander Archiv, Cologne; DACS, London, 2018. 77 © Estate of Otto Griebel. 68 © Marie-Louise von Motesiczky Charitable Trust 2018; presented by the Marie-Louise von Motesiczky Charitable Trust 2017, digital image © Tate, London, 2018. 81 Angela Pauser, Wolfgang Pauser. 9 (bottom), Chagall ®/ © ADAGP, Paris and DACS, London 2018; presented by Lady Clerk 1947, digital image © Tate, London, 2014. 84, 85 Musée d'Unterlinden, Colmar; © 2018 photo Scala, Florence. 6 (detail), 11 © Renata Davringhausen. 10 James Thrall Soby Bequest, acc. no.: 1213.1979; © 2018. Digital image, The Museum of Modern Art, New York/Scala, Florence, © DACS 2018. 31 John S. Newberry Fund, acc. no. 464.1967, © 2018. Digital image, The Museum of Modern Art, New York/Scala, Florence; © DACS 2018. 56, 57, 92, 93 reproduced with permission of Kunsthandel Widder, Vienna. 89 reproduced with permission of Kunsthandel Widder, Vienna; presented by Lord Duveen 1931, digital image © Tate, London, 2014. 40 (top left and bottom), 88 digital image © Tate, London, 2014. 39, 41 (left) © Estate of George Grosz, Princeton, N.J. / DACS 2018; presented by the Contemporary Art Society, 1955, digital image © Tate, London, 2014. 41 (right) © Estate of George Grosz, Princeton, N.J. / DACS 2018. 17 © Estate of George Grosz, Princeton, N.J. / DACS 2018, purchased with assistance from the Art Fund 1976, digital image © Tate, London, 2014. 36, 42 (detail), 67, Viola Roehr v. Alvensleben Muenchen.